D0849521

Japanese Literature in Chinese

[VOLUME I]

Poetry and Prose in Chinese by Japanese Writers of the Early Period

Prepared for the Columbia College Program of Translations from the Oriental Classics

Japanese Literature in Chinese

in Chinese

[VOLUME I]

Poetry & Prose in Chinese by Japanese Writers of the Early Period

Translated by Burton Watson

Columbia University Press   New York and London
1975

Library of Congress Cataloging in Publication Data
Main entry under title:

Poetry & prose in Chinese by Japanese writers of the early period.

(Japanese literature in Chinese; v. 1)
"Translations from the Oriental classics."
1. Chinese literature—Translations into English.
2. English literature—Translations from Chinese.
3. Japanese literature—Translations into English.
4. English literature—Translations from Japanese.
5. Chinese literature—Japanese authors—History
and criticism.   I. Watson, Burton, 1925–
II. Series.

PL2658.E1P6   895.1′1′008   75-15896
ISBN 0-231-03986-7

For Donald Keene
Who got me started on the subject

Contents

Part 1

INTRODUCTION

From very early times in their history the Japanese have written works of literature not only in their own language but in classical Chinese as well. Such works are known in Japanese as *kanshi* and *kambun*, which simply mean "Chinese poetry" and "Chinese prose" respectively, but here I would like to use these terms to designate specifically works of Chinese poetry and prose composed by Japanese writers.

In the present volume I have attempted to present a selection of the more interesting and important of such works dating from early times to the end of the Heian period—that is, from the middle of the seventh century to 1185. The first part of the book consists of poems by a number of different writers in the *shih* and *fu* forms, some brief prose tales from a Buddhist work entitled *Nihon ryōiki*, and one other prose piece. The latter part is devoted entirely to the poetry and prose of the greatest and most famous of the early Japanese writers of *kanshi*, Sugawara no Michizane (845–903). An appendix offers translations of a few of Sugawara no Michizane's *waka*, or poems in Japanese, for purposes of comparison.

Discussions of *kanshi* and *kambun* invariably raise several questions. One might first ask why the Japanese attempted to write at all in classical Chinese, a difficult language which few of them spoke and which in structure, word order, and mode of expression differs radically from their own.

The answer to this is not difficult to surmise. From the early centuries of the Christian era the Japanese had contact with China and the other states of the mainland which were within the sphere of Chinese cultural influence, and were no doubt impressed with the high level of material and spiritual civilization attained by the Chinese. They were further impressed when, at the end of the sixth century, the Sui dynasty succeeded in ending the long period of political disunion in China and uniting the country under a single powerful and highly centralized bureaucracy headed by the Son of Heaven. They were understandably eager to learn what they could from such a prestigious country and culture, and this involved mastering, in so far as possible, the language of that culture.

The states of the Korean Peninsula with which Japan was in close contact in this early period had already adopted classical Chinese as their medium for official documents and other types of writing, while the texts of Buddhism and Confucianism which they introduced to Japan were likewise couched in Chinese. And during the period from 607 to 894, when the Japanese court at frequent intervals dispatched official embassies to the Sui, and later to the T'ang, courts in China, the members of the embassy, as well as the students and monks who often accompanied them, were naturally required to have a knowledge of Chinese. The Chinese did not customarily deign to learn the languages of the various "barbarian" states which surrounded them, and such states were therefore obliged to learn Chinese if they were to participate in the culture of the Middle Kingdom, as China styled itself, and gain any recognition from it of their own cultural identity. Chinese was the language required for official communication with the mainland, as well as for any historical, philosophical, or literary works that one might hope to circulate on the continent. And, since diplomatic and social encounters were, in compliance with Chinese practice, accompanied by poems in Chinese of greeting, felicitation, and farewell, the Japanese had perforce to be able to produce such poems if they were to hold up their heads before the Chinese

4

and before the men of the states of the Korean Peninsula and Pohai in Manchuria, which followed Chinese custom.

Under these circumstances, it is only natural that the Japanese of the early period should have taken up the writing of *kanshi*, so that they could play their part with appropriate aplomb when in the presence of foreigners, and improve their skill and amuse themselves with the Chinese poetic medium when at social gatherings of their own kind. The same motives led them to produce numerous works in *kambun* or Chinese prose, some merely brief introductions or commemorative pieces, others works of great length and importance such as the *Rikkokushi* (six voluminous histories of early Japan that were compiled under official auspices), or the numerous commentaries and doctrinal writings of the Buddhist clergy.

Later, toward the end of the ninth century, as the Japanese gained greater confidence in their native culture and literature and as the T'ang dynasty, once so powerful, dwindled in prestige and eventually fell victim to internal dissension, both the need and the passion for composing works in Chinese declined. But the Japanese continued to write both poetry and prose in Chinese on occasion, presumably because by this time they had come to look upon the medium as part of their own literary heritage and continued to prize it for the ways in which it differed from their indigenous forms of expression. Both interest and competence, however, were by this time flagging, and these works in Chinese of the late Heian period are notably inferior to those of the early era, and hence are only sparsely represented in my selection.

The fact that the Japanese, in the youthful period of their history, devoted themselves so assiduously to the production of works of poetry and prose in a foreign language is of great sig-

5

nificance. Admirers of the indigenous culture, both in Japan and abroad, tend at times to view it as an unfortunate error of judgment, a diversion of energies and literary inspiration into a channel that was destined to produce results invariably imitative and strained. I prefer to take a more positive approach, admiring the men of the early period for their determination to transcend their insularity and participate to some degree in the larger sphere of Sinitic culture. I would like also to speculate on the advantages that may have accrued from such efforts. First of all, it is clear that the attempts of the Japanese to compose in a foreign language made them more conscious, and appreciative, of the characteristics and peculiar excellencies of their own language and literature. Further, it allowed them more readily to absorb Chinese literary devices such as parallelism, as well as Chinese literary themes and ideals, and to adapt them to the native literature. Though I can think of no major figure who excelled in both media, with the possible exception of Sugawara no Michizane, there were many competent writers who could at least handle both,[1] and it is clear that Chinese literature had the effect of refining the native tradition and making Japanese a richer and more effective medium for literary expression, just as Latin enriched the vernacular literatures of the various European states. In addition, it at times led to the creation of a certain number of deeply felt and important works of literature, works that probably would not have been composed in the native language, as I shall have occasion to remark on later.

Many people, including no doubt a number of those who

1. For example, 18 of the 64 poets represented in the *Kaifūsō*, the earliest anthology of *kanshi* (compiled in 751), are also represented in the *Man'yōshū*, the great anthology of Japanese poetry compiled shortly afterward, and it is even possible that the example of the former helped to inspire the compilation of the latter.

wrote them, seem to want to know whether the *kanshi* and *kambun* are sufficiently accomplished to pass for the work of Chinese writers if examined by Chinese critics. Not being a Chinese, I cannot hope to answer this question, nor indeed does it appear to me to be of all that great importance. Though there are notable exceptions, in general a writer attempting to express himself in a foreign language can seldom hope to do so with quite the confidence and dexterity of a native writer, and it is unreasonable to expect that the results will be of equal finesse.

More important, it seems to me, is to inquire whether the *kanshi*, and those *kambun* works with literary pretentions—regardless of how they might be viewed by Chinese critics—ever advanced beyond the level of mere imitations of mainland models or exercises in erudition, and if so, what particular characteristics and merits they display.

Before we can hope to answer this, we must consider what criteria are to be used in judging literary worth. Let us begin with one test that is relatively easy to apply, that of technical competence. Almost all the *kanshi* employ some variety of the *shih*, a predominantly lyric form which in most cases uses lines of five characters or seven characters in length and employs rhyme at the end of the even-numbered lines. All the works in the *Kaifūsō*, the earliest anthology of *kanshi*, are in the *ku-shih* or "old poetry" form, which means that they are unrestricted in number of lines and do not observe rules of tonal parallelism, though isolated couplets which do observe these rules are occasionally to be found. Later collections contain works in the newer forms such as the *lü-shih* and *chüeh-chü* that were beginning to replace the *ku-shih* in popularity on the continent. The *lü-shih*, or "regulated verse," is restricted to eight lines in length and observes elaborate rules of tonal parallelism. The *chüeh-chü* resembles the *lü-shih* but is only four lines in length. In addition to these, the Japanese also occasionally wrote works in the *fu* or rhyme-prose genre, a generally longer and freer form which is most often descriptive in nature and employs lines of varying lengths and rather ornate diction.

The Japanese, no doubt with the guidance of Korean and Chinese teachers and the help of rhyming dictionaries and other aids to composition, seem to have mastered rather rapidly the technical requirements of versification, and though occasional flaws and crudities are to be found, particularly in the early works, these may in some cases be due to faulty transmission of the text. The *kanshi*, to be sure, especially those of the later period, at times display oddities of word order or expression that are uncharacteristic of poetry composed on the continent and seem to be due to influences from the native language. Such oddities would no doubt draw disapproving frowns from Chinese readers, though whether they are from a technical point of view serious enough to affect the overall worth of the poetry I do not feel qualified to judge.

Since Chinese prose, unlike Chinese verse, is not governed by any set of technical rules, but depends for its effectiveness upon more subtle considerations of rhythm and euphony, it is more difficult to write with genuine grace. The quality of Japanese works of Chinese prose varies greatly with the particular writer and the content and purpose of the work. Some of the prose pieces in my selection are highly deft and polished; others, such as the Buddhist tales, so crude as to be barely intelligible in places.

To sum up these remarks on literary form, we may say that the Japanese, at least during the eighth and ninth centuries when they were in close contact with the mainland and when Chinese studies were in greatest vogue in court and intellectual circles, could write Chinese verse, and to a less extent Chinese

8

prose, with considerable competence, though understandably without any remarkable inventiveness or flair. Let us turn now to a consideration of the content and style of the works they produced.

It is important to note that the Japanese looked in upon the Chinese literary tradition at a time when interest and inspiration were at a rather low ebb. There had been much original, impassioned, and deeply reflective poetry both in the *shih* and *fu* forms written in the third, fourth, and fifth centuries, along with a great deal of verse that was, to be sure, merely decorative and pleasant. But tendencies toward pedantry and mannerism were already apparent, and with the sixth century, particularly among the writers of the Liang and Ch'en dynasties in the south, these tendencies came to predominate. The earlier subjectivity and passion, for reasons I can only guess at, abruptly disappear, and only superficiality remains. There are numerous works from this period celebrating gatherings and entertainments of the court and aristocracy, conventionally pious records of visits to Buddhist temples, and imitations of earlier *yüeh-fu* or folk ballads, but almost no poetry that is revelatory of the writer's deeper feelings or experiences. Even when the title of a work proclaims the poet's intention of pouring out his heartfelt emotions, the poem itself in most cases turns out to be curiously constrained and impersonal.

Though the Japanese were familiar with earlier and finer works through their study of the *Wen hsüan* and other standard Chinese anthologies, it was these currently popular poems of graceful but superficial description which in the earliest days they sought to imitate, celebrating the banquets and outings of their own court in the same flowery terms used by the Liang and Ch'en courtiers. My own selection from this period, since it for the most part avoids these merely ornamental pieces in favor

9

of the few works that seem to be sincerely felt, will no doubt give a false impression of the prevailing style of the period, but there would appear to be no point in translating banality simply to demonstrate that it exists.

This elegant but shallow style continued in vogue in China during the Sui and early T'ang and is reflected in the works of early Heian poets such as Emperor Saga and Fujiwara no Fuyutsugu. Around the middle of the eighth century, in the period known in Chinese literary history as the High T'ang, a brilliant group of poets, which includes such illustrious names as Wang Wei, Li Po, and Tu Fu, succeeded in revitalizing Chinese poetry and restoring to it the lost note of passion and moral and intellectual seriousness, but because of difficulties of communication in an age before the spread of printing, these innovations were slow to be recognized and appreciated by the Japanese. Meanwhile, another brilliant and highly popular poet named Po Chü-i (772–846) burst upon the scene. His works won wide acclaim on the mainland and were introduced to Japan during his lifetime, where their influence revolutionized the style and content of the Japanese *kanshi*. I shall have more to say concerning the exact nature of his impact when I discuss the poetry of Sugawara no Michizane, his most important follower in Japan. Here I will only note that his influence on the whole displaced earlier models and styles, and for the remainder of the Heian period, when Japan was cut off from direct contact with China, Po Chü-i's works remained the ideal both in poetry and prose. By this time the attention of the Japanese had turned from Chinese literature to the remarkable new genres and forms of expression that were evolving in their native language, and they no longer attempted to keep up with fashions on the continent. It may appear regrettable that, because of Po Chü-i's overwhelming popularity, the Japanese of this period did not fully come to appreciate the works of his immediate predecessors such as Li Po and Tu Fu, but these poets are stylistically more difficult than Po both to read and imitate, and it is not at all certain that their influence at this point would have been wholly salutary.

Before proceeding to an examination of the *kanshi* themselves, an interesting point may be noted about the relative length of Japanese and Chinese poetic forms. At the time when the first *kanshi* were written, the Japanese language had two principal poetic forms, the *tanka*, which was limited in length to 31 syllables, and the *chōka*, which resembled it in rhythm but was unlimited in length. For reasons which I am not competent to assess, however, the *chōka* subsequently dropped almost entirely out of use, so that the Japanese poet of the Heian period, if he wished to write in his native language, had virtually no choice but to confine his poetic utterance to 31 syllables. Chinese, as noted earlier, had some poetic forms that were limited in length, others that were not. The early *kanshi* poets chose in most cases to write brief works, perhaps because at this stage they lacked the confidence to undertake more sustained flights. But in the following centuries, as Japanese poetry grew shorter, the *kanshi* tended to grow longer, a fact that can scarcely be mere coincidence. Thus, for example, the "Song of the Tailless Ox" by Minamoto no Shitagō (911–983), on pp. 65–67, is made up of 42 lines of seven characters or syllables each, about the same length as the typical *chōka*. One wonders whether it would have been written in Japanese if the *chōka* had still been in fashion, or not written at all if the Chinese form had not been available to the writer. Both are possibilities that have important implications for literary history.

More important, and less in the realm of speculation, is the role which the *kanshi*, regardless of length, played as a vehicle for the treatment of certain themes that could not, or by convention would not, be treated in Japanese. Though there was greater thematic variety in early times, by the Heian period Japanese poetry seems to have been confined almost entirely to the subjects of love and nature, with a scattering of works in a religious vein. Ancient Japanese love poetry is justly famous for its psychological subtlety and great lyric beauty; it is significant that there are very few attempts to treat the subject of love in the *kanshi*, and that these few are purely conventional and impersonal imitations of Chinese models. The Japanese, it would seem, realized that for the expression of romantic sentiment, their native poetry was the superior medium. Nature, on the other hand, is treated extensively in the *kanshi* as well as in Japanese poetry, but here the treatment is so different in the two media that they appear to complement rather than compete with one another, the Japanese being elliptical and impressionistic, the Chinese direct, detailed, and customarily laid out in neat parallelisms. The poet could thus, depending upon which medium he selected to depict the beauties of the natural scene, create very different literary effects. Religious and philosophical musing are likewise to be found in both media, though the *kanshi*, because of its unlimited length, is clearly the more suitable vehicle for complex intellectual utterance. Finally, at least after the early period, it may be stated that Japanese poetry had become so restricted in theme that works dealing with politics, social criticism, the plight of the common people, or everyday family life could be treated virtually only in the *kanshi*.

This is not to suggest that all writers of *kanshi* took full advantage of the potential wealth of subject matter and freedom of length that the form offered. Most were content to venture nothing more ambitious than a pretty and conventionalized depiction of the scene about them, as the countless Heian *kanshi* on outings and visits to temples will attest. But, as I hope my selections will show, a few employed it to create serious and highly personal works of literature, and one of them, Sugawara no Michizane, produced in it poetry of such skill, variety, and power that he deserves to be numbered among the finest poets of his country.

Thus I would conclude that the early *kanshi* and *kambun* fulfilled three important functions. Though often no more than copy-book exercises in themselves, they served to facilitate the introduction of Chinese literary techniques and tastes into Japanese, and in doing so contributed to the growth and enrichment of the native tradition. At the same time they provided a medium for the expression of certain ideas and sentiments that could not easily be encompassed in the indigenous literary forms of the time. Finally, as I have pointed out above, they led on a few rare occasions to the creation of works that, far from being merely ancillary to the literature in the native language, are worthy to be counted among the indubitable masterpieces of the early period.

BIBLIOGRAPHICAL NOTE

My first acquaintance with the *kanshi* came some twenty years ago when, at the request of my friend Donald Keene, I undertook to translate a few examples for an anthology of Japanese literature which he was at that time compiling. These early efforts appeared in his *Anthology of Japanese Literature* (New York: Grove Press, 1955), and are for the most part reproduced here. At that time, however, I was very much a novice at the task of translating poetry in Chinese, and my ideas on how it should be done were somewhat different from those I now hold. I was, for one thing, much given to the use of inversions of normal English word order, being under the illusion, as Dr. Johnson said of some of his compatriots who employed such inversions, "that not to write prose is surely to write poetry." I have taken grateful advantage of the present opportunity to remove the more offensive of these inversions, as well as to make other minor revisions. In time I hope to produce a sequel to the present volume dealing with the *kanshi* and *kambun* of later Japanese writers, particularly those writers of late Tokugawa and Meiji times. I would like here to express my sincere thanks to the Asia Society for the assistance, granted through the Asian Literature Program under a grant from the National Endowment for the Humanities, which made the presentation of this selection of *kanshi* and *kambun* possible.

Below are brief bibliographical notes on the anthologies drawn upon in the first part of the book; bibliographical information on the works of Sugawara no Michizane will be found in the introduction to the second part.

1. *Kaifūsō* or "Fond Recollections of Poetry": Earliest extant collection of *kanshi* in one *kan* or chapter. Compiled in 751, it

contains over a hundred poems in *shih* form from the preceding eighty year period, arranged chronologically by author. It bears a preface in ornate and highly parallelistic *kambun* by the unknown compiler, imitative of Chinese models but regrettably lacking in specific information. The preface has been translated by Donald Keene, *Sources of Japanese Tradition* (New York: Columbia University Press, 1958), p. 88. Because the works of Prince Nagaya and his associates occupy such a prominent place in the anthology, it has been suggested that the compiler was a member of the literary coterie which centered about the Prince, a grandson of Emperor Temmu. The Prince was forced by accusations to commit suicide in 729 and many of his group were exiled, which may account for the fact that the compiler chose to remain anonymous. In making my versions I have consulted a number of modern Japanese studies and annotations of the text, but have not followed any single commentator throughout.

2. *Ryōunshū* or "Cloud-borne Collection": Anthology in one chapter compiled on imperial order by Ono no Minemori (778–830) and others, and containing 90 poems in *shih* form by Emperor Saga and other members of the imperial house and court bureaucracy composed during the period from 782 to 814, arranged by author. Preface in Chinese by Ono no Minemori.

3. *Bunka shūreishū* or "Collection of Literary Masterpieces": Anthology in three chapters compiled on imperial order by Fujiwara no Fuyutsugu (775–826) and others in 818. It contains some 140 poems in *shih* form arranged by subject. Preface in Chinese by Prince Nakao (early 9th cen.). The study and annotated text by Kojima Noriyuki in *Kaifūsō, Bunka shūreishū, Honchō monzui*, Nihon bungaku taikei #69 (Tokyo: Iwanami, 1964), is the basis of my translations.

4. *Keikokushū* or "Collection for the Ordering of the State": Anthology in 20 chapters compiled on imperial order by Yoshimine no Yasuyo (785–830) and others, and containing poetry in the *shih* and *fu* forms and prose works dating from the Nara period down to the time of compilation in 827, arranged by genre. Only six chapters are extant, Nos. 1, 10, 11, 13, 14, and 20 of the original; the first contains poems in *fu* form, the last, prose answers to questions set forth on the civil service examination, and the remainder poems in *shih* form. Preface in Chinese by Shigeno no Sadanushi (785–852).

5. *Denshi kashū* or "Collected Works of Mr. Shimada": Collection of the *kanshi* of Shimada no Tadaomi (828–891) in three chapters. The texts of the above five works are all to be found in *Gunsho ruijū* Vol. 6, *Bumpitsu*.

6. *Honchō monzui* or "Literary Gems of the Japanese Nation": Anthology in 14 chapters containing some 400 poems and prose pieces written over a period of 200 years or more and arranged by genre; compiled by Fujiwara no Akihira (989–1066), probably around 1060. My translations are based on the selection from the anthology contained in the work by Kojima Noriyuki cited in item number 3 above.

7. *Nihon shiki* or "Record of Japanese *Kanshi*": Collection in 50 chapters of all extant *kanshi* from earliest times to 1160, arranged by author, with annotations on sources, compiled by Ichikawa Kansai (1748–1820); modern printed edition in Kokusho kankōkai sōsho series (Tokyo 1911). For poems in more obscure late Heian collections, I have for the sake of convenience cited the chapter in which the poem appears in the *Nihon shiki*.

✍ Speaking My Thoughts

PRINCE ŌTOMO (647–672)

(Probably written after he had been appointed Prime Minister and heir to his father, Emperor Tenji. He reigned a brief seven months before being overthrown by his uncle, Emperor Temmu, and was not recognized as a legitimate sovereign until 1870, when he was given the posthumous title of Emperor Kōbun. The poem, one of the earliest of all extant *kanshi*, is couched in the archaic language of Chinese philosophy.)

✍ Virtue's way is to heed the canons of Heaven,
to lend salt and flavor to the food of Truth.
To my shame I lack the skill of praetor or guide—
how could I ever hold dominion over the four seas?

Approaching Death

PRINCE ŌTSU (662–687)

(Written when the Prince faced execution on charges of attempted rebellion.)

The golden crow [1] lights on the western huts;
evening drums beat out the shortness of life.
There are no inns on the road to the grave—
whose is the house I go to tonight?

1. Conventional term for the sun.

✍ Singing of the Moon

EMPEROR MOMMU (r. 697–707)

✍ Moon boat floats by misty shores,
its cassia oars drift past the haze-bound beach: [1]
across the terrace, clear torrents of radiance;
in our cups of wine, a sunken orb.
Waters have fallen—its slanting rays shatter;
trees are bare—its autumn light shines anew.
Alone this mirror among the stars
plies again the crossings of the Milky Way.

1. The opening lines may be taken to refer either to the boat in which
the emperor is seated as he enjoys the moonlight, or to the moon itself
as a boat drifting among the stars.

🖎 Watching Fish in the Water

KI NO SUEMOCHI (EARLY 8TH CEN.)

(The poem is taken almost verbatim from a work entitled "Poem on the Fishing Pole, *Yüeh-fu* Style," by the 6th century Chinese poet Chang Cheng-chien of the Ch'en dynasty.)

🖎 By the southern woods I have built my hut;
I drop my hook from the north lake banks.
Sporting birds dive as I draw near;
green duckweed sinks before my gliding boat.
The quivering reeds reveal the fish below;
by the length of my line I know the water's depth.
With vain sighs I dangle the tempting bait
and watch the spectacle of avaricious hearts.

⚞ In Tᾱng China Longing for Home

PRIEST BENSHŌ (EARLY 8TH CEN.)

(Ch'ang-an, literally, the city of "Long Rest," is the T'ang capital, where the priest had been sent to study; the poem plays on the repetitions in each line.)

⚞ Sunrise I look to the source of the sun,
among clouds seek where the clouds begin;
a distant journey, weary in a distant land,
Long Rest—for me only the pain of long sorrow! [1]

1. The journey to China was perilous and many who undertook it were lost at sea or succumbed to illness abroad. The following poem by the Chinese poet Hsiang Ssu (mid-9th cen.) is entitled "The Ailing Japanese Monk" and describes one visitor to China who in all probability never lived to make the journey back. *San-t'i-shih* ch. 3.

> "Clouds and water block the way home,
> though when I came, winds blew the ship along—"
> He says nothing of what to do if he should die,
> but, sick as he is, still sits in meditation.
> Deep walls swallow up the light of the lamp,
> open windows air out the moxa smoke.*
> "Dreams of home are ended now—
> make my grave by the temple gate."

* The monk is taking moxa treatment for his illness.

✍ Autumn Day at the Home of Prince Nagaya; a Banquet for the Envoy from Silla

ABE NO HIRONIWA (658–732)

(Prince Nagaya (d. 729), grandson of Emperor Temmu, was a poet and patron of the arts. Silla was one of the states on the Korean Peninsula which maintained close relations with Japan.)

✍ Mountain windows scan the deep valley;
groves of pine line the evening streams.
We have asked to our feast the distant envoy;
at this table of parting we try the pleasures of poetry.
The cicadas are hushed, the cold night wind blows;
geese fly beneath the clear autumn moon.
We offer this chrysanthemum-spiced wine in hopes
of beguiling the cares of your long return.

✍ Written When Appointed Commander of the Western Sea Marches

FUJIWARA NO UMAKAI (694–737)

✍ Last year service in the eastern hills,
this, the marches of the western sea.
How often in the span of an official's life
must he weary himself with these border wars?

✍ *In early spring, while at the temple at Bamboo Ravine Mountain (Tsuge), I received word of a banquet at the home of Prince Nagaya. I sent the following by way of excuse*

PRIEST DŌJI (D. 744)

✍ Cleric black and layman white are plainly far apart,
in truth as hard to mix as lacquer and gold.
Monk's robes will hide this shivering frame,
patched begging bowl fill a hungry gullet.
I twist vines to fashion a hanging curtain,
pillow my head on a stone, lie down among cliffs.
I've made off with my body, far from worldly cares;
cleansing my mind, I hold fast to the True Void.
Propped on a staff, I climb the spiring crags,
spread the breast of my robe, let the gentle breeze blow in.
Clean and cold, the snow of peach petals;
vast and vacant, Bamboo Ravine Mountain—
though willows, surprised by spring, have already changed hue,
a lone man still feels the last of the cold.
Monk that I am, already removed from realms of men,
what business would I have showing myself in banquet halls?

✍ Fujiwara no Nakamaro, Governor of Ōmi, wrote a poem on the two willows at the place where his deceased father had practiced meditation on Mt. Hiei; I wrote this to match his poem

ASADA NO YASU (EARLY 8TH CEN.)

(Ōmi, on Lake Biwa at the foot of Mt. Hiei, was the site of the capital in the time of Emperor Tenji (r. 662–671). Some editors treat the piece as two poems, the first ending with line ten.)

✍ Ōmi, emperor's city,
Hiei, surely a sacred mountain;
the mountain is still, all worldly dust hushed,
its valleys idle, given wholly to Truth.
He, your ancestor, august one,
alone, enlightened, began his good karma here.
The precious hall perched overlooking air,
temple bells borne down the wind,
mist and clouds, a scene ten thousand years old,
pine and cypress hale through winter's ninety days—
but sun and moon come and go, come and go;
his model of loving kindness alone endures.
This place where in stillness he practiced meditation,
suddenly its flagged court is rank with weeds!
Old trees, bare in the last of autumn,
cold grasses withered now ninth month is here—
all that remains—two willows
where dawn and evening the filial son mourns.

25

⚘ Sitting Alone in the Mountains

THE RECLUSE TAMI NO KUROHITO (DATES UNKNOWN)

⚘ Mist and fog shroud out the dust of the world,
mountain and stream embellish the place where I live.
At a time like this, should I turn to scribbling poems,
the breeze and moon would surely look down on me with
    scorn! [1]

1. Something of the textual uncertainties of the *Kaifūsō* may be indi-
cated by the fact that the third line, if one follows another version,
comes out meaning: "At a time like this, should I fail to produce a
poem."

FOUR TALES FROM THE *NIHON RYŌIKI*

The *Nihon ryōiki*, the full title of which is *Nihonkoku gempō zennaku ryōiki* or *Miraculous Stories of Karmic Retribution of Good and Evil in the Land of Japan*, was written in *kambun* by Kyōkai, a monk of the Yakushi-ji in Nara. Almost nothing is known about the author, but the work was apparently compiled around 787 and enlarged over the years up to 822. In three chapters, it is a collection of anecdotes, modeled on Chinese works of the Six Dynasties and early T'ang, which extol Buddhist teachings and illustrate the miraculous powers of various Buddhist deities and the workings of the law of karma. Crude and graceless in style, it nevertheless has a disarming directness and charm, and exercised a great influence on later Japanese collections of tales. A complete English translation and study of the *Nihon ryōiki* by Kyoko Motomochi Nakamura has recently been published under the title *Miraculous Stories from the Japanese Buddhist Tradition*, (Cambridge: Harvard University Press, 1973).

In Worshipping Chinese Gods He Killed Oxen as a Sacrifice, but He also Did Good by Setting Living Things Free, and He Received Both Good and Evil Reward (Chapter Two, Section Five)

Once in the province of Settsu, the district of Higashinari, in the village of Nadekubo, there lived a master of a rich household. His name is not known, but the time was the reign of Emperor Shōmu (724–748). This rich man worshipped Chinese gods and used to pray to them and make offerings. Each year he would slaughter an ox as a sacrifice.[1] At the end of seven years, having thus killed seven oxen, he was suddenly seized with a severe illness that lasted for seven years. The doctors tried various remedies but to no effect. The rich man summoned diviners and magicians to perform charms and exorcise the evil, but his illness only grew worse. Thinking that his malady had perhaps come about because he had taken life, the man from the time he first took to his bed observed without fail the six fast days of each month and set free all his living creatures. When he learned that anyone else was taking the life of living beings, he immediately ransomed them at whatever price was asked, and he sent men here and there to buy all living things in captivity and free them. At the end of seven years, he knew that his time had come and he summoned his wife and children and said to

1. In 791 the government issued an order prohibiting persons from slaughtering oxen and using them in the worship of Chinese gods, so the cult was apparently fairly widespread; animal sacrifice was almost certainly foreign to Japan and was of course particularly abhorrent to persons of Buddhist belief.

them, "After I die, set my body aside for nineteen days [2] before you cremate it." Accordingly, his wife and children laid his body away and waited for the end of the nineteen days, but when only nine days had passed, the man returned to life and told them this story:

"There appeared to me seven beings who had the heads of oxen and the bodies of men. They tied ropes to my hair and dragged me along with them. As we went, I saw a palace with tall towers. 'Whose palace is that?' I asked, but the creatures only looked at me with eyes full of hatred and pushed me on, saying 'Hurry up!'

"When we had entered the gates of the palace, they announced, 'We have summoned him!' and I realized that this was the palace of Yama, the King of Hell. The King asked the demons, 'Is this your enemy, the man who killed you?' 'This is he!' they answered and brought out a carving board and small knives. 'Give your judgment quickly, we pray, for we wish to carve him up and eat him the way he did us!' they said.

"But just then a host of over ten million persons appeared and untied the ropes that bound me, saying, 'This man is without blame! He did injury only because of the gods he worshipped.' Then they placed me in the middle and every day the seven demons and the multitude of men argued and contested back and forth like fire against water. King Yama tried to arrive at a decision but could not determine which side was in the right. The demons pressed their case with fury, saying, 'It is perfectly clear! This man made himself our master, cut off our four legs and prayed in the hall of worship for his own profit. He chopped us into bits and ate us up. We ask only that now we be

---

2. Some versions of the text read "nine days;" customarily cremation was carried out on the day of death.

allowed to butcher and eat him in the same way!' But then the great multitude would plead with the King, saying, 'We know perfectly well that this man is without blame. The blame rests with the gods and spirits he worshipped!'

"The King pondered and decided that the evidence rested with the majority and on the evening of the eighth day he issued his royal command: 'Tomorrow come again before me!' On the ninth day, in obedience to his order, we all again came together and King Yama pronounced his decision: 'Justice has been made clear. We shall abide by the evidence of the majority.'

"When the seven oxen heard this, they began to lick their lips and drool, making motions of chopping something and devouring it. With wrathful looks they raised their knives and cried, 'Will you give us no recompense for our wrong? We will not forget it and someday we will have our revenge!'

"Then the great host of people surrounded and protected me and led me out of the palace. They placed me in a carriage and lifted it on their shoulders, raising banners and bearing me onward; they saw me off with shouts of praise and knelt in reverent farewell. All the members of this multitude were alike in appearance, and I said to them, 'Honored sirs, who are you?' They answered, 'We are the living things that you ransomed and set free. We have not forgotten your goodness and now we have come to repay you.' "

After the rich man had returned from the halls of King Yama, he made a vow that he would no longer in any way serve the strange gods and spirits but would put all his faith in the Three Treasures.[3] He tied a holy pennant to his rooftop and converted his house into a temple, placing an image of the Buddha within,

---

3. The Buddha, the Dharma or Doctrine, and the Sangha or Buddhist Order.

practising the Law, and setting free living creatures. From this time on, his house was known as the Nade Hall. His illness never returned and he lived to be full of years, dying at the age of over ninety.

Having Ransomed Some Crabs and Set Them Free, She Was Rewarded by Being Saved by Them (Chapter Two, Section Twelve)

In the province of Yamashiro, in a community in the district of Kii, there was a young woman of unknown name who was tender-hearted by nature, believed firmly in the law of karma, observed the five precepts and the ten good deeds, and never deprived any living thing of life. In the reign of Emperor Shōmu, some of the cowherds in the village where she lived caught eight crabs in a mountain stream and were about to roast and eat them. The young woman, seeing this, pleaded with the herdboys, saying, "Please be so kind as to give me the crabs!" but the boys refused to heed her, replying, "We're going to roast them and eat them!" Earnestly she begged and entreated them, taking off her cloak and offering it in payment, and finally the boys handed over the crabs to her. She then requested the Dhyana Master Gi to perform prayers asking for merit, and set the crabs free.

Sometime later, the young woman went into the mountains and there came upon a huge snake about to swallow a large frog. She said to the snake imploringly, "If you will only give me that frog, I will present you with numerous offerings of woven goods!" When the snake ignored her and refused to listen, she promised to gather together even more woven goods and pray to him, saying, "I will worship you like a god if you will heed my pleas and release the frog!" The snake paid no attention, however, and went on swallowing the frog. Then she said to the snake, "If you will give me the frog I will become your wife, so please let it go!" With this the snake at last took notice of her, lifting up its head, stretching out its neck, and peering into the young woman's face. Then it spat out the frog and let it go. The woman thereupon arranged an assignation with the snake, saying, "Come to me when seven days have passed."

Later she told her father and mother all about the incident with the snake. They were distraught and said, "You are our only child! How could you have been so insane as to make impossible promises like that!"

At this time the Eminent Monk Gyōgi [1] was in residence at the Jinchō-ji in the district of Kii, and so the young woman went and reported to him what had happened. When he had listened to her, he said, "Ah, what an astounding story! The only thing to do is to have faith in the Three Treasures!"

Having received his instruction, she returned home, and when the night for the assignation arrived, she shut the house up tight and prepared to defend herself, making various religious vows and placing her trust in the Three Treasures. The snake circled about the house, slithering this way and that on its belly and pounding against the wall with its tail. Then it climbed up onto the roof, chewed a hole through the thatch, and dropped down in front of the young woman. But before it could approach her, there was a sudden outburst of noise, with sounds of scrambling, biting, and chewing. The next morning when the young woman looked to see what had happened, she found eight large crabs gathered there, and a snake that had been hacked and slashed into little pieces.

If even such lowly and unenlightened creatures know how to repay a debt of gratitude when they have incurred it, how can it

1. 668–749, a priest of the Hossō Sect who was renowned for founding temples, preaching, and devoting himself to bettering the lot of the people.

be right for human beings to forget the debts they owe? From this time on in the province of Yamashiro great honor was paid to the large crabs that live in the mountain streams, and it was considered an act of goodness to set them free.

⚰ The Eminent Monk Gyōgi, Seeing that the Child a Woman Was Carrying Was Her Enemy from a Past Existence, Had Her Throw It in the River, Whereupon it Manifested a Wonder (Chapter Two, Section Thirty)

The Eminent Monk Gyōgi opened up the Naniwa River Canal, set up ferry crossings, preached the Dharma, and converted the people. Monks and laymen, eminent and humble all gathered about him to listen to the Dharma. On one such occasion in the province of Kawachi, the district of Wakae, the village of Kawamata, there was a woman who, carrying her child in her arms, went to take part in the religious meeting and listen to the Dharma. But the child began to wail and complain so that she could not hear the sermon. The child was already over ten years old but had never learned to walk and did nothing all day but wail and scold, suck the mother's milk and eat.

The Eminent Monk Gyōgi addressed the woman, saying, "Fie, young lady! You must take your child and throw it in the depths of the river!" When the crowd heard this they put their heads together and began to whisper, saying, "The holy man is usually so compassionate—what possible reason would he have for making a pronouncement like that!" The woman, being of loving nature, did not throw away the child but continued to hold it in her arms and listen to the sermon.

The following day she came once more with the child in her arms to hear the Dharma, but this time the child wailed so vociferously that the entire crowd of listeners was prevented from hearing the sermon. The Eminent Monk Gyōgi berated the woman, saying, "Throw that child in the river!" The woman began to grow suspicious and, unable to put her doubts out of her mind, finally threw the child into the deepest part of the river. The child floated to the surface of the water, where it kicked its feet, flailed its arms, glared with wide staring eyes, and said in a tone of great disappointment, "What a pity! I wanted to keep on eating off you for three years more!"

The mother, more suspicious than ever, returned to the meeting to listen to the Dharma. "Have you thrown the child away?" the Eminent Monk Gyōgi asked. The woman in reply told him all that had happened. "In a past existence," he explained to her, "you borrowed something from that person and failed to pay it back, and so the person took on the form of a child and was trying to get back at you by eating so much. That child was none other than the owner of the goods!"

Alas, how shameful for the woman! One should never die without paying back one's debts to others, for if one does, one will surely meet with some reprisal in a future existence.

An Orphan Girl Pays Respect to a Bronze Statue of Kannon and Receives Recompense in a Miraculous Manner (Chapter Two, Section Thirty-four)

In a village near the Uetsuki Temple in the western sector of Nara there lived an orphan girl who as yet was unmarried; her family and given name are unknown. When her father and mother were alive, the family possessed great wealth, built numerous houses and storerooms, and cast a bronze image of the bodhisattva Kannon, two feet five inches in height, erecting a sanctuary some distance from the main house in which the statue was enshrined and worshipped. But in the time of Emperor Shōmu the young woman's parents passed away, the servants all ran off, and the horses and oxen died. The former wealth vanished, the household was reduced to poverty, and the young woman, all alone in her empty mansion, did nothing but sigh and shed sorrowful tears day and night. Hearing that pleas addressed to the bodhisattva Kannon were likely to be answered, she tied a cord to the arm of the bronze statue and, taking it in her hand and making offerings of flowers, incense, and lights, she prayed for good fortune, saying, "I am an only child, an orphan without father or mother, living all alone in a poor house without wealth or means to support myself. I pray you to grant me a happy lot! Grant it quickly, send it soon!" she said, weeping and imploring day and night.

In the same village there lived a rich man who had lost his wife. Seeing the girl, he dispatched a matchmaker to arrange for her to become his bride. But the girl said to the matchmaker, "I am now impoverished and do not have so much as a cloak to cover my naked body! Where would I get a veil for my face so that I could appear before him and speak in his presence?"

The matchmaker returned and reported this to the man who, on hearing it, replied, "I am perfectly aware that she is poor and has no proper clothes. But will she marry me or not?" The matchmaker conveyed his words to the girl. She persisted in her refusals, but the man went and forced his way into the house, coaxing her until her heart softened and she consented to sleep with him.

The following day it rained all day, and the rain continued so that the man was unable to return to his own home and had to remain at the young woman's house for three days. Growing very hungry, he said, "I'm starving! Bring me something to eat!"

"I will prepare something at once," his bride replied. She built a fire in the stove, set the empty rice steamer on it, and crouched beside it, pressing her cheeks in her hands; she wandered this way and that through the empty rooms, sighing loudly. Then she rinsed her mouth, washed her hands, went to the sanctuary and, taking hold of the cord that was tied to the statue, wept and said, "Do not let me be put to shame! Send me some wealth right away!" When she had finished speaking, she left the sanctuary and returned to the kitchen, squatting before the empty stove as before, her cheeks pressed in her hands.

The same day, at the hour of the monkey,[1] there was a sudden rapping at the gate and the voice of someone calling. When the young woman went to see who it was, she found the wet nurse from the rich family next door. The nurse was carrying a large wooden box filled with a hundred different things to eat

1. Around four in the afternoon.

and drink, every conceivable delicious flavor and aroma, all in vessels of metal or lacquer. Handing the box to the young woman, she said, "We heard that you had a guest and so the mistress next door fixed these things to bring to you. Just be good enough to return the dishes when you're finished."

The young woman was delighted beyond measure and, her heart overflowing with gratitude, she took off the black cloak she was wearing and gave it to the nurse, saying, "I have nothing but this grimy cloak to offer, but I hope you will be kind enough to accept it." The nurse took the cloak, put it on, and hurried off home. When the young woman served the dishes to her husband, he looked at the food in astonishment and then, taking his eyes from the food, stared at the face of his bride.

The following day the man took his leave and later sent his wife ten bolts of silk and ten bales of rice, saying, "Sew the silk into robes as soon as you can and quickly make some wine from the rice." The young woman went to the rich house next door to tell them of the happiness in her heart and express her gratitude and respect, but the mistress of the house said, "Have you gone mad, child, or are you perhaps possessed by devils? I have no idea what you are talking about!" The nurse added, "Neither have I!"

Scolded thus, the young woman returned to her house and, as was her custom, went to the sanctuary to pay her respects. There she saw the black cloak which she had given to the nurse draped over the bronze statue, and for the first time realized that it was Kannon who had aided her. As a result, she came to believe in the law of karmic retribution and, doubling her devotions, treated the statue with even greater respect and reverence than before. Thereafter she regained the wealth that her family had once possessed and was freed from hunger and fret. She and her husband, spared from illness, lived in health to a great old age. This indeed was a wondrous affair.

✍ Rhyme-prose on the Small Hills

ISONOKAMI NO YAKATSUGU (729–781)

(Though the writer belongs to the Nara period, the poem is preserved
in a Heian collection, *Keikokushū* ch. 1, and for purposes of convenience
is here grouped with the Heian works.)

✍ How the four seasons march in succession
Unwaywardly, from ages past!
Grasses that greet the spring in flowered tapestry;
The summer trees curtained in leaves;
In the sad breath of autumn, the falling fruit;
Bare branches before the shrill winter wind—
When I see these seasonal things, I know
That man too must flourish and die.
I have heard of the hills of Paradise but never seen them;
Toward the land of the gods I gaze, not knowing the way.
I know only that to make a mountain
You must pile the little clods one by one.
Where then should I seek nobility?
In what delights the heart there is nothing mean.
I roof the narrow grotto in the garden end,
Lead the thin stream to flow before my hall.
Hills beneath heaven,
On the broad earth, trees—
These things that the small man spurns
The wise will cherish.

Though I want in the straits of distress,
How should I decline the defenses of virtue?
At my ease I dip from the lakes of the west;
My gaze governs the northern waters.
And these ragged hills
That shut not out the coursing sun;
This clear bright pond,
Ruffled in the wind;
Pines that nod from their crags in greeting;
Rocks shining from the river bottom beneath drifting watery
    mirrors;
Scattered clouds that cloak the summits in shadow;
The half-risen moon that lights the vales,
When from tree to tree dart crying birds:
To these I will abandon, entrust my life.
The Great Creator in the variety of his works
Blesses as well the lowly and small.
When all philosophy I resolve in this one act,
I may stride the leviathan seas and they will not hold me;
Into the dark heart of all being I will ride
And dwell in the spacious halls of the ant.
Truly one need not seek beyond his door for wisdom;
Must a man see all mountains and seas to love them?
To these lines I have entrusted
The writing of what my heart has learned.

Reprise:
Four seasons taking leave in turn,
Ten thousand things that flower and fade;
Look to the past, a different age,
And you will know that the future will walk the same road.
True loftiness lies in the heart;

41

The narrowest plot is sufficient for me.
Pure, serene, I leave all to fate;
Mountains of the immortals are nothing to me.
Though I do not flock with others,
What need to hide from the world altogether?
Contented with gourd and lunch basket fare,[1]
I will contrive to live out my years.
To act but look for no return—
Who understands this virtue?
I live in peace, indifferent,
The Tao to be my only rule.

1. The simple food in which, according to the *Analects*, Confucius's
foremost disciple Yen Hui found contentment.

✍ At a Farewell Party for Fujiwara no Yoshino, Sub-official of Mino

EMPEROR JUNNA (R. 824–833)

(Written in 813, some years before Emperor Junna came to the throne; Fujiwara no Yoshino had been assigned to duty in the province of Mino. The poem is interesting for the bravado with which it attempts to transcend the traditional Chinese and Japanese attachment to place, though it is noteworthy that it is not the writer but the recipient of the poem who is obliged to make the journey to a far off land. *Bunka shūreishū* ch. 1.)

✍ Suddenly tonight we must say goodby:
I never thought we'd be whirled apart like falling petals,
beyond the white clouds a thousand miles away—
but don't fret—for a man, any place is home!

⍋ Spring Dawn by the River

EMPEROR SAGA (R. 810–823)

(Date uncertain. Written when Emperor Saga was on an outing to the
Kaya detached palace beside the Yodo River at present day Yamazaki;
see p. 99. *Bunka shūreishū* ch. 1.)

⍋ In a lodge by the river, far removed from affairs of men,
pillow pushed aside, all I hear are cock crows from the old fort.
Cloud breath that dampens my robe tells me crags are near; [1]
stream sounds startling my sleep make me realize how close the
  valley is.
Lone moon at the sky's edge rides the river's swift flow;
hungry monkeys deep in the hills wail till break of day.
Though seasonal signs caution us warm weather is still far off,
by banks and shoals, spring grasses are ready to turn lush and
  green.

1. According to ancient Chinese belief, clouds were produced by the
caves and crags of mountains; Kaya was at the foot of Mt. Tennō.

⚰ Weeping for the Priest Gempin

EMPEROR SAGA

(Gempin, who died in 818 around the age of eighty, was originally a
monk of the Kōfuku-ji in Nara. Distressed by what he regarded as a
lack of true religiosity there, however, he retired and lived most of his
life in the mountains. He was highly respected at the early Heian court.
Bunka shūreishū ch. 3.)

⚰ The Great Man from time past had no fixed abode,
in famed mountains hid his traces, grew old amid wind and
   frost.
Weary long ago of worldly dust, he took on cleric form;
now returned to the crux of Truth, suddenly he's vanished.
Pines shade his old hut, dense and green as before;
grasses darken his new monument, already grown rank and desolate.
Rush mat he used when alive, left empty in the moonlight;
now he's gone, who will offer incense in the golden burner?
In the Forest of Meditation, branches break, trunks topple now
   and then,
But the Dharma Halls will long mourn the loss of this pillar and
   beam.
Priests and laymen alike grieved; now their rites are ended.
We bow in reverence to a place far away, facing a westward direction.[1]

---

1. The direction of the Western Paradise, realm of the Buddha Amida.

✍ Spring Day in a Mountain Lodge

PRINCESS UCHIKO (807–847)

(Composed when her father, Emperor Saga, visited the Kamo Shrine, where she was a priestess, in the spring of 823. *Zoku Nihon kōki*, Kōnin 14th yr.; *Nihon shiki* ch. 4.)

✍ Silent was my lonely lodge among the mountain trees
when to this lakeside your fairy carriage came.
The lone forest bird tasted the dew of spring;
cold flowers of the dark valley saw the sun's brightness.
Springs sound close by like the echo of early thunder;
hill hues shine tall and clear when evening rain has passed.
If I should once more know the warmth of this fair face,
all my life I will give thanks to the azure skies.

Hearing Flutes along the Road in the Autumn Night: to Match a Poem by the Director of the Imperial University Sugawara no Kiyotata[1]

FUJIWARA NO FUYUTSUGU (775–826)

(*Ryōunshū*)

A feel of autumn in the tall sky of dusk;
hastening officials, through at court, descend from the palace.
In the new night strolling players sound their flutes,
the long notes, the short notes, that stir men's thoughts.
Wind from the willows bears the cry of a *luan* bird,
the moon in the ash tree lights the figure of a phoenix:
soon we'll hear such music as they played for the sage Shun
when the birds and beasts danced in his royal city! [2]

1. The grandfather of Sugawara no Michizane; his personal name may also be read Kiyotomo.
2. So great was the virtue of the ancient Chinese ruler Shun that various auspicious birds and beasts, such as the phoenix and *luan* bird mentioned here, gathered in his capital and danced. The allusion implies a graceful compliment to the Japanese rulers under whom Fuyutsugu served, especially Emperor Saga, during whose reign, we know from the evidence of Emperor Saga's poems, the poem above was written.

✍ *After a long time in the provinces, I returned to my old school in my late years, but all my friends were gone and I couldn't find anyone I knew, so I wrote this to express my feelings.*

HAYASHI NO SABA (EARLY 9TH CEN.)

(*Ryōunshū*)

✍ In late years returning to my old school:
old acquaintances—how many have taken leave!
Things as they were, but not the same men today;
a time when sorrow comes, joy departs.
To forget the trap with, no old friends; [1]
tipping carriage tops in greeting, new faces now.
I wanted to talk about old times,
but suddenly I couldn't hold back the tears.

1. "The fish trap exists because of the fish; once you've gotten the fish, you can forget the trap. . . . Words exist because of meaning; once you've gotten the meaning, you can forget the words. Where can I find a man who has forgotten words so I can have a word with him?" *Chuang Tzu* sec. 26.

48

⬡ On a Winter Day Drinking Wine at a Friend's House in the Country

I NAGASHIRO [1]

(Keikokushū ch. 13)

⬡ A house where the long embankments are old,
fine fields west of it and east:
to enter I stroll among willows,
cross a moat to reach the guest hall.
Ice has bound the moat, its ripples stilled;
frost has fallen, leaves are all gone,
but still there's plenty of wine and lute-playing,
all in the manner of the Bamboo Grove. [2]

1. "I" is probably an abbreviation for some surname or place name; nothing is known of the writer or of the moated grange which is the scene of the poem.
2. Where the so-called Seven Sages of the Bamboo Grove, a group of Chinese philosopher-poets of the late 3rd century, gathered to drink, play the lute, and discuss philosophy.

🖋 Banished from the Palace, I have recorded something of my feelings and respectfully present them with a letter to the Palace Guard Yoshimine no Yasuyo.

PRINCE NAKAO (EARLY 9TH CEN.)

(*Bunka shūreishū* ch. 1) [1]

🖋 Wine and feasts I followed with the host of officials;
unworthy, yet I stood in the Court of the Emperor.
With reverence I received the rites of investiture—
next day to be banished from the council chamber!
On that noble ground, no room for my anxious feet;
from high heaven came accusations—to whom could I cry?
I left the company of the virtuous, the ranks of the adorned;
to me alone the sea-encircling dew came not. [2]
I listened outside the palace to the sound of singing;
below the stairs, apart, watched the dancing girls on the terrace.
I returned in the dusk to face my wife in shame;
through the night I lay talking with my children in bed.

1. This translation is one of those made some twenty years ago and, under the title "The Banished Official," was published in the Keene *Anthology* cited earlier. Though somewhat freer than my more recent translations, it is in no way basically inaccurate, and I have decided to reproduce it with only minor revisions.
2. That is, imperial favor; metaphors relative to the sky, sun, dew, etc. in Chinese and Japanese poetry often refer to the ruler.

Great faults and small merit were mine, I know;
for mercy and light penalty I am forever grateful.
Though I may never again enter the gate of my lord,
I shall speak from this far land and Heaven may hear me.

𝄢 Washing My Hair

SHIMADA NO TADAOMI (828–891)

(*Denshi kashū* ch. 1)

𝄢 I look at the comb, look at the water, look at what has
    fallen;
age and youth are far apart, I cannot have them both.
Don't tell me that my hair gets thinner by the day—
see instead how the beards of my grandsons grow out!

52

✍ Rhyme-prose on the Marriage of Man and Woman

ŌE NO ASATSUNA (886–957)

(*Honchō monzui* ch. 1. The rhymes used in this *fu* or poem in rhyme-prose form spell out a sentence reading: "Love and emotion bring mutual response, and afterwards the body becomes pregnant (full)." The piece is typical of the mildly erotic works which, under Chinese influence, were occasionally composed by Japanese of the period. Presumably the juxtaposition of elegant and erudite language in which they were cast and the earthiness of the theme produced a contrast that readers of the time found titillating. The *Honchō monzui* (ch. 12) includes a far more explicitly salacious piece entitled "Biography of Iron Hammer," a life history of a phallus by someone who writes under the alias of "Organ Extraordinary." Interesting as it may appear in conception, however, it turns out in execution to be one of the most tedious works of pornography in all literature, and accordingly has not been translated here.)

✍ Most virile of beings—man;
Gentlest creature—woman:
Their love and affection will find a way to mingle,
No matter how parents may prohibit and protect.
First he solicits the matchmaker,
Skilled in all the art a glib tongue can command,
Then plies her with Japanese poems,
Bit by bit tangling the strings of her heart.
He seeks a glimpse of her face, so hard to see,
Listens for a voice as yet unheard.
As his yearning grows more fervid, he smiles in secret;
As the talks grow more intimate, he feels his heart break.

53

"Like the jeweled tree in my garden,
Like the faithful pine," he gestures, "I vow to flourish!
Like the felicitous herbs in my room,
Like the golden orchid," he points, "I promise to be pure!"
And now bodies grow subtly mild,
Their wills little by little aroused,
She dwelling in loveliness,
In charms a match for Ono no Komachi,
He speaking with a quiet elegance
That would shame Ariwara no Narihira.[1]
Their longings begin to race forth wildly;
True passion now is born.
Her form resplendent, replete with all beauty,
Her posture tall and stately, with power to topple cities;[2]
She dyes her crimson sleeve in a hundred scents
Till he has fallen slave to their fragrance;
Wraps her white fingers tight about his hand
And already he is lost in mazes of emotion.
A woman values her chastity,
The completion that comes with the marriage rite;
But when they've vowed to be true for a thousand years,
She finds joy in the first night's union.
When the dew of dawn gathers,

1. The poetess Ono no Komachi (fl. ca. 850) was famous for her
beauty, the poet Ariwara no Narihira (825–880) for his handsome looks
and finesse as a lover.
2. A reference to the lines in the poem attributed to Li Yen-nien of the
Former Han:

> "Beautiful lady in a northern land,
>   standing alone, none in the world like her,
>   a single glance and she upsets a city,
>   a second glance, she upsets the state!"

It wets her fresh new garments;
Where night's pale moonlight falls,
It lights her soft shining form.
Her eyebrows painted in willows of Wei,
Lips touched with rouge of Yen,
Where once she hung silk curtains about her,
Bashful lest even her kin catch a glimpse,
Now she turns the gauze lamp to the wall
And suddenly snuggles up to a stranger.
What at first she only endures
Later becomes most familiar.
Unbinding the sash of her single robe,
Knowing she cannot tie it again,
Baring flesh white as snow,
Forgetting for once to be ashamed:
"He's the one I'm to be buried with,
The mate I will share through all my life!"
When the form is lovely, love will be deep,
When passion penetrates, the body will grow full:
Not the union of husband and wife alone that counts,
But the thought of sons and grandsons to rely upon!
He broaches the gate where moisture abounds,
And fluids overflow to stain their undergarments;
They look about, but there's no one at the door:
Moans grow louder, impossible to still.
Love's raptures are hard to forbear—
Who among us is a saint or sage?
The mutual response of yin and yang,
This is the Creator's natural way.
And when hearts have subsided and rest in stillness,
They linger by Peachflower Paradise banks, forgetting to return;
After juices have freely flowed,

They lie wrapped in dreams of a Heaven of Perfect Peace.
But thoughts once roused know no end,
And longings may leave one sleepless and distraught;
Should widows and young boys hear of such things,
None but would be stirred to desire!

✍ Record of the Pond Pavilion

YOSHISHIGE NO YASUTANE (D. 997)

(The city of Kyoto, which became the capital of Japan in 794, was laid out in the form of a neat rectangle in imitation of the Chinese city of Ch'ang-an, capital of the T'ang dynasty, with the imperial palace in the north and a broad thoroughfare, Suzaku-ōji or the Avenue of the Vermilion Bird, running south from the palace gate and dividing the city into eastern and western sectors. To make room for the new city, the course of the Kamo River, which had originally cut through the center of the site, was shifted to the east, so that it ran south along the edge of the eastern sector. In spite of government measures designed to make the citizens dispose themselves with appropriate symmetry on either side of the central avenue, the western sector seems for various reasons to have been unpopular from the first and, as will be seen, grew increasingly deserted through the years. In addition, because the Kamo had been forcibly shifted out of its natural course, and also perhaps because the aristocracy were cutting down trees to build estates along the upper reaches of the river and its tributaries, the city was troubled by frequent floods. The following piece touches upon these problems that beset the city—as well as that of the urban sprawl that was developing in the eastern and northern suburbs and depriving the citizens of their customary recreational areas—before settling down to a description of the author's own home and the spiritual peace he found there. The piece is especially interesting for the resemblance which it bears to the famous Japanese classic by Kamo no Chōmei (1153–1216), the *Hōjōki* or *Account of My Hut*, and the influence which it undoubtedly exerted on Chōmei's work. *Honchō monzui* ch. 12.)

For the past twenty years and more I have observed the situation throughout the eastern and western sections of the capital. In the western part of the capital the houses have become fewer and fewer till now it's almost a deserted wasteland. People move out of the area but no one moves in; houses fall to ruin but no new ones are ever built. Those who don't have any other place to move to, or who aren't ashamed to be poor and lowly, live there, or people who enjoy a life of obscurity or are hiding out, who ought to return to their native mountains or countryside but don't. But anyone who hopes to pile up a fortune or whose heart is set on rushing around on business wouldn't be able to stand living there even for a day.

In years past there was one mansion there, with painted halls and vermilion doors, groves of bamboo and trees, rocks and fountains—a spot so superb it was like a different world. But the owner because of some affair was sent into exile,[1] and fire broke out and burned the buildings down. There were thirty or forty families of retainers living nearby, but one after another they moved away. Later the owner of the house returned but he never tried to rebuild, and though he had many sons and grandsons, they didn't remain in the area for long. Thorns and brambles grew till they covered the gate, and foxes and wildcats dug their burrows there in peace. From all this it is clear that it is Heaven which is destroying the western sector and no fault of men.

In the eastern sector of the capital, particularly in the area northeast and northwest of Shijō, there are huge crowds of people living, eminent and lowly alike. Towering mansions are lined up gate by gate, hall in sight of hall; little huts have only a wall between them, eaves all but touching. If a neighbor to the east suffers a fire, neighbors to the west seldom escape being burned out; if robbers attack the house to the south, the house

1. Minamoto no Takaakira, a high official who in 969 was demoted and assigned to a post in the Dazaifu in Kyushu; he was allowed to return to Kyoto in 972.

58

to the north can't avoid the shower of stray arrows. One branch of a family living south of the avenue is poor, another branch north of the avenue is rich, and though rich relatives may have no special virtue to boast of, poor relatives still must suffer shame. Then there are the humble folk who live in the shadow of some powerful family: their roof is broken but they don't dare thatch it, their wall collapses but they don't dare build it up again; happy, they can't open their mouths and give a loud laugh; grieving, they can't lift up their voices and wail; coming and going always in fear, hearts and minds never at rest, they're like little sparrows in the presence of hawks and falcons. And how much worse when some great mansion is first built and then begins bit by bit to broaden its gates and doors, swallowing up the little huts all around. Then how many of the poor people have occasion to complain, like sons forced to leave the land of their father and mother, like officials of paradise banished to the dusty world of men. In the worst cases, so great is the squeeze for land that a whole family of poor commoners ends up by being wiped out.

Again, there are those who elect to build their houses along the eastern bank of the Kamo, but if a bad flood comes along, they find themselves keeping company with fish and turtles. Others move out into the fields to the north, but if a drought occurs, they may perish of thirst before they find any water. Aren't there any plots of empty land left within the two sectors of the capital to settle in? Why do people have to be so stubborn?

Along the river and in the fields to the north they not only build row on row of houses, but also lay out vegetable gardens and rice paddies, the old gardener settling down on the land and piling up ridges between the fields, the old farmer constructing embankments along the river and leading water into his paddies.

59

But year after year now there have been floods, the river over-flowing and breaking down the levies, and officials charged with keeping the river in check who yesterday boasted of their achievements today leave the breaks sitting as they are. Do they expect the citizens of the capital to turn into fish?

I have privately checked into the regulations and find that in the area west of the Kamo, only the Sūshin-in is permitted to have rice fields; in all other cases they are strictly prohibited because of the danger of flood damage.[2] Moreover, the area east of the river and the northern fields represent two of the four suburbs of the capital, where the Son of Heaven goes to greet the seasons or to enjoy an outing. If people take it on themselves to build houses there or start growing things, why don't the authorities prohibit and put a stop to it? What about the ordinary citizens who would like to stroll about and amuse themselves? Summer days when people want to enjoy the cool, they find there are no more banks where they can fish for little ayu trout; in the autumn breeze when gentlemen want to go off hunting, they find there are no more fields where they can loose their young falcons. Season by season people scramble to move out of the city, and day by day the area within the capital becomes more deserted, until the wards in the southern section are turned into a vast wilderness of weeds, where only "the ears of grain droop down."[3] Leaving the rich and fertile lands, peo-

2. The Sūshin-in or Cloister for Honoring Relatives, a home for indigent females of the Fujiwara clan founded by a member of the family in 860, was situated in a low-lying area at Gojō Kyōgoku. The regulations which Yasutane refers to prohibited the constructing of rice paddies along both the east and west banks of the Kamo.

3. Reference to a poem in the *Shih chi*, "Hereditary House of Sung," which describes the desolate appearance of the former capital of the Yin dynasty.

ple go off to barren and stony ground. Is Heaven causing this as well, or is it the madness of men themselves?

Originally I had no house of my own, but stayed in someone else's house at the Jōtō Gate. Constantly aware of the disadvantages of such an arrangement, I decided I didn't want to live there forever, and in fact, even if I had wanted to, it would have been impossible. Estimating that I could buy two or three *se* [4] of land for ten million cash, I finally chose a barren plot north of Rokujō, where I put up a wall on four sides and constructed a gate. I selected the kind of out-of-the-way spot that Prime Minister Hsiao would have approved of, and at the same time aimed for the clean, spacious grounds of Chung-ch'ang T'ung.[5] In all, my land measures some ten or more *se*. Where the ground is high I made a little artificial hill, in the sunken part I dug a small pond. West of the pond I built a small hall to house the Buddha Amida, east of the pond put up a little building to hold my books, and north of the pond constructed a low house for my wife and children. In general the buildings cover four-tenths of the area, the pond three-ninths, the vegetable garden two-eighths, and the water-parsley patch one-seventh.[6] In addition I have an island with green pines, a beach of white sand, red carp, white herons, a little bridge and a little boat. Everything I've loved all my life is to be found here. In particular I have the willows on the eastern bank, in spring misty and lithe; in summer the bamboos by the northern door, clear breezes rustling through them; in fall the moon in the western window, bright

4. One *se* is approximately equal to one are, 100 square meters or 119.60 square yards.
5. References to the estates of the Chinese statesmen Hsiao Ho of the 2nd cen. B.C. and Chung-ch'ang T'ung of the 2nd cen. A.D.
6. Yasutane's figures clearly aim more at verbal neatness than mathematical accuracy.

enough to read a book by; and in winter the sunlight by the southern eaves, just right for warming my back.

So, after five decades in the world, I've at last managed to acquire a little house, like a snail at peace in his shell, like a louse happy in the seam of a garment. The quail nests in the small branches and does not yearn for the great forest of Teng; the frog lives in his crooked well and knows nothing of the vastness of the sweeping seas. Though as master of the house I hold office at the foot of the pillar, in my heart it's as though I dwelt among the mountains.[7] Position and title I leave up to fate, for the workings of Heaven govern all things alike. Heaven and earth will decide if I live a long life or a short one—like Confucius, I've been praying for a long time now.[8] I do not envy the man who soars like a phoenix on the wind, nor the man who hides like a leopard in the mists. I have no wish to bend my knee and crook my back in efforts to win favor with great lords and high officials, but neither do I wish to shun the words and faces of others and bury myself away in some remote mountain or dark valley. During such time as I am at court, I apply myself to the business of the sovereign; once home, my thoughts turn always to the service of the Buddha. When I go abroad I don my grass-green official robe, and though my post is a minor one, I enjoy a certain measure of honor. At home I wear white hemp garments, warmer than spring, purer than the snow. After washing my hands and rinsing my mouth, I ascend

7. At this time Yasutane held the post of *naiki* or secretary in the Nakatsukasa-shō, a bureau of the government which handled imperial edicts, petitions, and other documents. "Clerk at the foot of the pillar" was the Chinese term for such a secretary.
8. When Confucius fell ill, one of his disciples asked to be allowed to pray for him, but Confucius replied, "I've been praying for a long time now." *Analects* VII, 34.

the western hall, call on the Buddha Amida, and recite the *Lotus Sutra*. When my supper is done, I enter the eastern library, open my books, and find myself in the company of worthy men of the past, those such as Emperor Wen of the Han, a ruler of another era, who loved frugal ways and gave rest to his people; Po Lo-t'ien of the T'ang, a teacher of another time, who excelled in poetry and served the Buddhist Law; or the Seven Sages of the Chin, friends of another age, who lived at court but longed for the life of retirement.[9] So I meet with a worthy ruler, I meet with a worthy teacher, and I meet with worthy friends, three meetings in one day, three delights to last a lifetime. As for the people and affairs of the contemporary world, they hold no attraction for me. If in becoming a teacher one thinks only of wealth and honor and is not concerned about the importance of literature, it would be better if we had no teachers. If in being a friend one thinks only of power and profit and cares nothing about the frank exchange of opinions, it would be better if we had no friends. So I close my gate, shut my door, and hum poems and sing songs by myself. When I feel the desire for something more, I and my boys climb into the little boat, thump the gunwale and rattle the oars. If I have some free time left over, I call the groom and we go out to the vegetable garden to pour on water and spread manure. I love my house—other things I know nothing about.

Since the Ōwa era (961–964), people of the time have taken a fancy to building luxurious mansions and high-roofed halls, even going so far as to have the tops of the pillars carved in the shape of mountains and duckweed designs incised on the sup-

9. Emperor Wen reigned 179–157 B.C.; Po Chü-i (772–846), whose poems were greatly admired in Japan and whose prose pieces in fact provided the model for the present work by Yasutane; on the Seven Sages of the Bamboo Grove, see p. 49, n. 2 above.

ports of the roof beam.[10] But though the expenditure runs into many millions in cash, they manage to live there barely two or three years. People in old times used to say, "The builder doesn't get to live in what he builds"—how right they were. Now that I am well along in years, I've finally managed to construct a little house, but when I consider it in the light of my actual needs, even *it* seems somewhat too extravagant and grand. Above, I fear the anger of Heaven; below, I am ashamed in the eyes of men. I'm like a traveler who's found an inn along the road, an old silkworm who's made himself a solitary cocoon. How long will I be able to live here?

Ah, when the wise man builds a house, he causes no expense to the people, no trouble to the spirits. He uses benevolence and righteousness for his ridgepole and beam, ritual and law for his pillar and basestone, truth and virtue for a gate and door, mercy and love for a wall and hedge. Devotion to frugality is his family business, the piling up of goodness his family fortune. When one has such a house to live in, no fire can consume it, no wind topple it, no misfortune appear to threaten it, no disaster come its way. No god or spirit can peer within it, no thief or bandit can invade. The family who lives there will naturally grow rich, the master will enjoy long life, and office and rank will be with it forever, to be handed down to sons and grandsons. How can one fail, then, to exercise caution?

> *Composed and written in the hand of the master of the house,*
> *Yasutane, in the tenth month, the first month of winter, of the*
> *fifth year of Tengen (982).*

---

10. The latter part of the sentence is a conventional Chinese expression indicating architectural extravagance and should not necessarily be taken literally.

⚖ Song of the Tailless Ox

MINAMOTO NO SHITAGŌ (911–983)

(Shitagō was well known as a writer of Japanese verse and was one of
the compilers of the officially sponsored anthology *Gosenshū*. Prevented
by the overweening power of the Fujiwaras from advancing in the
world, he often complained in his Japanese verse, as in the following
work in Chinese, of his poverty and lack of recognition. *Honchō monzui*
ch. 1.)

⚖ I have an ox but its tail is missing;
everyone pokes fun at my tailless ox.
Born a wild calf, it was chewed by a wolf,
but I well understand why it escaped the wolf's jaws:
it's so wise you'd take it for an old pine spirit,[1]
far plumper and bigger than those grazers under the fruit trees.
And though it lacks a tail, it has five virtues;
with your leave, I'll rap its horn and count them one by one.
    (first virtue)
First, when it eats tender grass and turds come flopping down,
it has no tail to swish about and dirty up the shafts.
    (second virtue)
Should it stray into a garden and rouse the owner's ire,
there's nothing he can tie a dead ox skull to.[2]
    (third virtue)

1. Reference to a Chinese legend concerning the spirit of an ancient
pine tree that turned into a gray-green ox.
2. A note by the poet explains that if an ox wanders into a garden, the
owner of the garden will tie an ox skull to its tail and make it run several miles.

Again if it mingles with herds of cows in the broad meadow,
the herdboy can spot it far off without searching about.
　　　(fourth virtue)
Black ox with dots of white hair on its back—
a wise man of old examined it and caught the thief.[3]
But in your case, to seize the scoundrel, determine the thief,
what need to scrutinize and report on hair?
Even a short tail might omen long life for the culprit,
but with you he's certain to end up in chains.
　　　(fifth virtue)
Other people's sons and daughters race about in carts,
off on long trips to mountain temples, short ones to market tav-
　　　erns,
sometimes not returning till dusk or even the following day,
wearying the ox, wearing down the wheels, worrying the owner.
But because my ox has no tail, no one wants to borrow it—
though others laugh in scorn, I have no cares.
Tailless, tailless, hark to what I say!
Never have I used you to plow paddy or field,
nor driven you east and west, fetching and hauling,
and the rare times you hauled a load, I charged no fee.
It's not that I can't bear to see you put to work;
poor, I've forgotten how to make a living at farming or trade.
Old now, I stick to my post, though the stipend's skimpy,
and number in my household no lackey or groom.
In grass green spring I have no sleek horse to straddle,

3. According to a Chinese work, a man had a black ox with white
markings on its back which was stolen. The magistrate thereupon offered to pay double the regular price for ox hides, and when one of that
description was brought to him and identified by the owner of the ox,
the thief was arrested.

in snow white winter I've trouble patching together a proper
   cloak.
True, you're here to pull me, but is that such a comfort?
Tailless, tailless, do you know what I mean?
While we serve a wise sovereign, we live for loyalty, not wealth!
That's why I get up early, rest but little at night.
And if my worthless loyalty should win some paltry return,
tailless, I'll surely pay you for your years of hard work!

✍ Death Bed Poem

PRIEST JAKUSHŌ (LATE 10TH CEN.)

(Zoku-ōjōden; Nihon shiki ch. 34)

✍ In the grass hut no one to help me up;
fire in the incense burner, I sleep facing west.
Flutes and songs far off I hear above the lone cloud:
sacred hosts coming to greet me before the sinking sun.

✍ The Puppeteers

FUJIWARA NO TADAMICHI (1097–1164)

(The *kairaishi* or puppeteers were a gypsy-like people who wandered about Japan making a living by singing, dancing, operating puppets, and performing feats of magic. *Hosshōji Nyūdo shū; Nihon shiki* ch. 48.)

✍ Ceaseless wanderers from of old, the puppeteers,
over countless miles always seeking a new home.
They set up camp and sing alone in the night to the autumn
  moon;
restless, they seek new paths in the mist of spring fields.
Youth in the bright capital, their women pampered favorites;
the years of age alone, watching over a hut of thatch.
The traveler passing far off casts suspicious eyes
at the white hair, the vacant, wrinkled face.

Part 2

POEMS AND PROSE

OF

SUGAWARA NO MICHIZANE

INTRODUCTION

Sugawara no Michizane was born in 845, the third son of Koreyoshi, a court scholar in the Kyoto of the early Heian period. Exceptionally bright and diligent, he passed the entrance examination to the state university in 862 and completed the literature course in 867, entering upon a career as a teacher and court official. At some uncertain date previous to this, he had married Nobukiko, the daughter of one of his father's students, Shimada no Tadaomi, and began raising a large family. He advanced rapidly in the bureaucracy and soon was renowned for his skill in writing poetry and prose in Chinese.

Chinese studies, encouraged by a succession of erudite emperors, were at the height of their popularity. Japanese envoys and monks journeyed to the mainland, Chinese came to Kyoto, and classical Chinese was the language used for all state or scholarly papers. Officials like Michizane were chosen from among candidates who had passed examinations in Chinese studies modeled after those of the T'ang bureaucratic system. Government and private schools in the capital, staffed by men like Michizane's father, tutored the sons of the aristocracy in the reading and composition of Chinese.

Like his father, Michizane became a distinguished teacher, and his poetic works contain an interesting series of poems written in 883 to congratulate ten of his students on passing the government examination, in which he praises the younger ones for their precocity and comforts the older ones—one man had apparently been trying most of his life to pass—with the reminder that, in Lao Tzu's words, "great vessels are a long time in the making." His students by custom remained loyal to their teacher and his interests after they entered government service, and for this reason Michizane and his clique soon came to pose a serious threat to the power of the Fujiwara family, who dominated the court and maintained a school of their own. It is not surprising to find, therefore, that in 886 Michizane was appointed governor of the province of Sanuki, in northeast Shikoku, and dispatched from the capital.

Michizane no doubt regretted leaving the cultured society of Kyoto, though he seems to have done his best to be a conscientious provincial administrator. Interestingly, he did not, like so many Heian aristocrats, complain of the crude and uncouth ways of the country, at least in his poetry. Instead, in the best humanist tradition of the great T'ang poets, he composed poems depicting the hardships of the common people.

Back in the capital in 890, he rose rapidly in office and imperial favor, and in 894 was accorded the highest recognition as a scholar of Chinese by being chosen to head a diplomatic mission to the T'ang court. Surprisingly enough, after receiving the appointment, he almost immediately submitted a memorial advising the suspension of all such missions to the Chinese mainland. As with many of Michizane's actions, we can only guess at his true motives. His apologists claim that, for all his Chinese learning, he realized that Japan no longer needed to seek leadership or cultural guidance from the continent; his detractors, on the other hand, suggest that he did not, for private political reasons, wish to absent himself from the capital, or that he suddenly lost his nerve at the prospect of the perilous sea journey. No one denies that travel to and in China at this time was dangerous, and that the political situation on the continent was highly unsettled—the T'ang dynasty was overthrown eleven years later. It is quite possible, therefore, that Michizane acted neither out of fear nor scheming ambition, but with the best interests of his country at heart when he suggested that a dangerous, expensive, and possibly fruitless diplomatic mission be canceled. In any event, the mission was called off and he never got to China; like the great Japanese sinologues of the Tokugawa era, he died without ever having visited the country whose literature and culture he spent a lifetime studying.

Michizane continued to rise in power until, by 899, he held one of the highest posts in the government, that of Udaijin or Minister of the Right. This was a dangerous height, and one which his rivals at court could no longer tolerate. In the first month of 901, he was abruptly accused of various treasonable acts and ordered into exile at the Dazaifu, a government office in northern Kyushu. We will never know the real facts of the case, since nearly all the documents pertaining to it were deliberately destroyed shortly after his death. But certain circumstances surrounding the move, including the fact that Emperor Daigo's father, the Retired Emperor Uda, under whom Michizane had served with distinction, was prevented from appealing on his behalf or even examining the charges, suggest that they were dubious at best. Michizane's wife and most of his numerous children were forced to remain in the capital or were exiled elsewhere. Only the youngest son and daughter, still in their childhood, were permitted to accompany their father in the long journey west which, according to the poet, required over fifty days to complete.

Life at the Dazaifu in Kyushu would have been hard even for a man unaccustomed to the comforts of the capital. The official quarters assigned to Michizane, an old lodge built for the use of foreign envoys, were a shambles, and he was often without adequate supplies of food or fuel. He suffered from beriberi, stomach trouble, and skin rashes, probably as a result of malnutrition, and the loneliness of exile was deepened by the death of his little son about a year after his arrival. Weakened by privation and broken in spirit, he himself died early in the spring of 903 at the age of fifty-eight.

Death, and the circumstances under which it comes, can do strange things to a man's reputation. Not many years after Michizane passed away in Kyushu, a series of disasters fell upon the capital—persistent drought and plague, the premature death of several of Michizane's old rivals of the Fujiwara clan, the demise of two crown princes in succession. To the men of the time, it seemed obvious that the angry spirit of Michizane was exacting its revenge, and steps were hurriedly taken to appease it. Michizane was restored to his former position and title and accorded other posthumous honors, and when these moves failed to put an end to the strange happenings, a shrine was set up in the area in the northwest sector of Kyoto called Kitano or North Field where offerings were made to him under the title Temmangū Tenjin. In time other shrines were established to pay him honor, until his cult became spread throughout Japan.

It is ironic that the mild and bookish Michizane should have been worshipped first as an *onryō*, a spirit of wrath and vengeance. But fear of the supernatural was a very real part of Heian life, and the men of the time believed that an unjust death could work terrible changes in the soul. It was not long, however, before the memories of Michizane's distinguished career, rather than his tragic end, began to dominate the popular conception of the god Tenjin. In time, the man who had lectured on Chinese historical texts, written a learned preface to a treatise on Buddhism by the famous monk Ennin, compiled works on Japanese history, and won acclaim for his poetry in Chinese and Japanese,[1] became recognized as the patron deity of literature and learning. At a much later date, he also came to be revered as

1. On Michizane's poetry in Japanese, see Appendix.

76

the god of calligraphy, though there is little historical evidence to indicate that he excelled in that art. Perhaps the strangest cult associated with his name is that which arose among the Zen monks of the Muromachi period who, like Michizane, were enthusiastic students and writers of Chinese verse. They declared that he had in fact visited China and there studied Zen under a master of the Sung dynasty—founded half a century after his death. They even produced pictures of him as he appeared in dreams, wearing the cap of a Taoist immortal, the robes of a Zen priest, and carrying a branch of his favorite flower, the *Prunus mume* or plum.[2]

Michizane's grandfather Kiyotata had journeyed to T'ang China in 804 as a member of an official embassy, traveling in the same ship as the famous Buddhist monk Saichō, and spent a year on the mainland, and one of Michizane's uncles had been official envoy to China. His family thus had direct and personal knowledge of the continent, and he himself had occasion to meet

2. Though the anachronisms of this view are only too obvious, one should not suppose that the Zen monks were totally irresponsible in their pronouncements. In a long poem written in 901 ("Recording My Thoughts"), Michizane says: "Turning my mind about, I study and practice Zen," and though "Zen" here undoubtedly designates some kind of Tendai or Shingon meditation practice, one cannot blame the Zen monks for regarding it as a kind of proto-Zen. In addition, as poems such as that written in 889 entitled "*Kōjin* Night: Relating My Thoughts" indicate, he carefully observed the Taoist custom, common among the Heian aristocracy, of sitting up all night on the night of the sixty day cycle with the designation *kōjin*, because it was believed that on such nights, if one slept, the "three spirits" within the body would escape and report one's misdeeds to the Emperor of Heaven. Of his love for the plum his poems give ample evidence, and the plum tree today is an invariable fixture in shrines dedicated to his worship.

visitors to the capital from China and the state of Pohai, which was situated north of Korea. It is probable that he read Chinese texts in Chinese word order and with the current Chinese pronunciation, though whether he spoke Chinese we do not know. His writings in Chinese, however, show traces of what are known as *washū*, certain idiosyncrasies of usage and word order peculiar to the Chinese poetry and prose written by Japanese.

His 514 extant poems in Chinese are contained in two collections, the *Kanke bunsō*, a work compiled in 900 by Michizane himself and consisting of twelve chapters, of which the first six are devoted to poetry; and the *Kanke kōshū*, a work in one chapter containing the remainder of his poems, principally those written during his exile in Kyushu. Some of his poems are cast in the eight-line *lü-shih* or four-line *chüeh-chü* forms so popular in China at this time, which observe elaborate rules of verbal and tonal parallelism; others are in the freer *ku-shih* or "old poetry" form. Many are public in nature, being composed at official banquets and ceremonies, often on themes set by the ruler. Others, more personal in tone, deal with Michizane's relations with his family, friends, and students, or the events of his daily life. It is from this latter category that I have chosen the works translated here, because they are clearly motivated by deep emotion and reflect the poet's actual experiences and feelings. Such a method of selection may give a somewhat distorted impression of his personality, suggesting that he was forever voicing worries and grievances, which is by no means the case. However, he wrote in a tradition that regarded poetry, when it was not simply a graceful ornament to social occasions, as principally a vehicle for the expression of sorrow, and moreover seems himself to have been a man of rather melancholy temperament. The reader will note, for example, how many of his longer poems start out in a rather light hearted manner but in the end sink into a mood of despair. Adversity in the end destroyed him, but it also, ironically, inspired his finest poetry.

The latter six chapters of the *Kanke bunsō* contain a few works in the *fu* or rhyme-prose form, and Michizane's prose writings in Chinese. Most of these are official documents of one kind or another and hence of mainly historical interest. I have, however, translated one descriptive piece dealing with his library which sheds interesting light upon his teaching and scholarly activities.

Like most Japanese writers of Chinese poetry and prose in Heian times, Michizane was profoundly influenced by the works of the Chinese poet Po Chü-i (772–846), who was known in Japan as Po Lo-t'ien or Haku Rakuten. Arthur Waley has even gone so far as to describe Michizane's indebtedness to Po's works as a case of "literary prostration," though this judgment strikes me as excessive.[3] There are several obvious reasons why Po's collected works, the *Po-shih wen-chi* or *Hakushi monjū*, enjoyed such popularity from the time of their introduction to Japan early in the ninth century. First of all, Po's poems had won wide and rapid acclaim in China during the poet's lifetime, and the Japanese could thus feel assured that they were reading works that the Chinese themselves valued highly. Secondly, Po employed a relatively simple, though elegant, style, and his writings were thus comparatively easy to read and imitate, particularly in comparison to those of other more difficult T'ang masters such as Tu Fu. Thirdly, many of Po's best poems are engagingly intimate and relaxed in tone, conveying to the reader a distinct sense that he is being brought into real and meaningful contact with a fellow human being. At the same time, Po also wrote poetry of social protest in which he described the lives

3. Arthur Waley, *The Nō Plays of Japan* (London: Allen and Unwin, 1921), p. 248.

and hardships of the common people. Such poems, introduced into the aristocratic society of Heian Japan, had a novelty and tone of moral and social seriousness that no doubt compelled the Japanese to reexamine their concepts of the nature and function of poetry and inspired some of them, such as Michizane, to write poems of a similar nature on the common people of their own land.[4] Finally, Po was, unlike most eminent Chinese poets, a confessed Buddhist and writer of devotional poetry, and this made him particularly attractive to men like Michizane who, though by profession teachers of Confucian learning, were in private life ardent followers of the Buddhist faith.

Some of the most admirable qualities in Michizane's poetry—the note of intimacy and emotional sincerity, the sensitivity to social ills, the relaxed, simple style he often employs—are traceable, I believe, to Po Chü-i's influence. At the same time he is clearly a very different person from Po Chü-i, more fretful and morose in temperament, more deeply dependent upon the solace of his religious faith, and, as shown by the poems of his period of exile, less able to rise above the misfortunes which fate dealt him. Also, as he himself confesses, he could not find in wine the comfort which Po and so many other Chinese poets claimed to find but, particularly in his late years, drank only to be sociable or, at the urging of his family, in hopes of easing his physical ills.

In the end, the remarkable thing about Michizane's poetry in Chinese is not the degree to which it succeeds in resembling the verse of native Chinese, but the degree to which it is distinc-

4. Other examples are the poems "Observing the Woman Charcoal Seller" (*Nihon shiki* ch. 4) by Prince Sukehito (late 11th cen.), third son of Emperor Go-Sanjō, and "The Old Man Selling Charcoal" (*ibid.* ch. 49) by Fujiwara no Tadamichi (1097–1164), both clearly inspired by Po Chü-i's "New *Yüeh-fu*" poems.

tively his own. Through the medium of Chinese verse he manages to convey a deep sense of himself, and we come away from his works feeling that we know him more intimately and manifoldly than we know most of the poets of his time who wrote only in Japanese. Eventually the medium in which he wrote ceases to be important, and all that matters is the miraculous way in which the experiences of a man who lived in Japan over a thousand years ago become accessible to us today.

TRANSLATOR'S NOTE

For a number of years I have been attempting to read Michizane's poetry, though with only indifferent success due to the lack of adequate commentaries and background material. The excellently annotated text of the *Kanke bunsō* and *Kanke kōshū* by Kawaguchi Hisao, *Nihon koten bungaku taikei* #72 (Iwanami 1966), now fills this deficiency, and I acknowledge it with gratitude as the basis of my translations. For historical material in the introduction I have also drawn on Sakamoto Tarō, *Sugawara no Michizane, Jimbutsu sōshō* #100 (Yoshikawa kōbunkan 1962). *Sugiwara no Michizane to Dazaifu Temmangū* (Yoshikawa kōbunkan 1975), 2 vols., appeared too late to be utilized in my study; the first volume consists of essays by various scholars on Michizane's life and work.

POEMS AND PROSE OF
SUGAWARA NO MICHIZANE

⬩ In Late Winter Visiting the Palace Gentleman Bun (Fun'ya) and Enjoying the Early Plum Blossoms in His Garden: Preface to a Poem

(*Kanke bunsō* 1)

Recently the government issued an order prohibiting the drinking of wine, and since its promulgation, no one has disobeyed.[1] So unless I call on old acquaintances or visit close friends, I have no way to enjoy a cup of wine and indulge in the writing of poetry. Old acquaintances are not necessarily close friends, and close friends are not necessarily old acquaintances, but the Palace Gentleman Bun happens to be both. Poets are not necessarily drinking companions, and drinking companions are not necessarily poets, but again the Palace Gentleman Bun happens to be both. I and my group, five or six of us, happened to catch the Palace Gentleman on his day of rest, and so for a while we are able to enjoy ourselves with wine and poetry. Calculating the progress of the year, we find that the worst of the winter cold is drawing to a close, and examining the trees in the gar-

1. In the 1st month of Jōgan 8 (866) the Council of State, complaining of the prevalence of drunken brawls and disorders among the officials and nobles, issued an order prohibiting drinking at large gatherings; small groups of friends could get together to drink provided they first obtained permission from the government.

83

den, we discover ourselves in the presence of flowering plums. Seasons that are hard to come by should be properly appreciated; things that are quick to fade away deserve to be cherished. So now that we have gathered here with our old acquaintance, should we not write poems on the early blossoms of these fragrant trees, and perhaps let the associates of our old acquaintance know that this is the way things are done among the followers of Confucian learning?

✍ I Give up Trying to Learn to Play the Lute [1]

(*Kanke bunsō* 1)

✍ I was certain that lute and calligraphy would help my
    studies,
idle seasons beside the window, seven stretched strings—
but no concentration of mind brings improvement—I squint in
    vain at the score,
fingering so confused I keep having to ask the teacher.
My choppy "Rapids" never has an autumn river sound,
my frigid "Raven" no sadness of a nighttime cry.
Music experts all inform me I'm merely wasting time—
better stick to the family tradition, writing poems!

1. The *koto* or horizontal lute, called in Chinese *ch'in*. The poem was
probably written around 870.

✍ Sitting in a Circle, Speaking Our Thoughts

(Michizane drinking with student friends at his home; he was only about twenty-four at the time, but already speaking with an amusingly professorial tone. *Kanke bunsō* 1)

✍ Before we know, the year passes, so many stumbles!
What's to be done but gather in a circle?
Wine to forget sorrow—have plenty of cups!
Poems to pour out thoughts in—lots of paper here.
I'm ashamed that in young days I rattled around on pointless errands,
always regret that with my spear I cannot turn back the evening sun.
My ideas, your feelings—let them all out tonight,
and tomorrow when you go home, don't waste time!

✍ Grieving for the Student Abe

(Kanke bunsō 1)

✍ Who doubts the world is a thing of wind and waves—
what use to cry in pain to the blue sky?
Teaching and learning we did in those days all ended now—
For you I turn west, intone Amida's name.[1]

---

1. The Buddha Amida, Lord of the Western Paradise.

◢ Through the Snow to Early Duty at the Office

(*Kanke bunsō* 1)

◢ Wind wafts palace bells sounding the hour of dawn;
I hurry along the road through tumbling flurries of snow.
Clad in my three foot coat of fur,
mouth nicely warmed with two portions of wine,
I wonder if the chilly groom has daubed willow fluff on his
  collar,
amazed to see my tired horse tramping through drifting clouds.
At the office, no time for a moment's rest;
huffing on my hands a thousand times, I scribble official drafts.[1]

---

1. In the 2nd month of 874, when this was written, Michizane was appointed *suke* or assistant in the Mimbushō, an office in charge of affairs pertaining to the populace.

✍ I Stopped along the Road to Look at the Old House of Lord Minamoto and Was Moved to Write This.

Lord Minamoto passed away at the end of last summer, and a few months later fire broke out in one of the garden pavilions.[1]
(*Kanke bunsō* 2)

✍ In one morning burned to the ground—the old estate;
earnestly I ask what's happened to the orphans he left.
Patterned tiles, broken and burnt, among hues of old moss;
half charred pines where bird voices call;
they say that moldering grasses will change into fireflies;
alas, that these blackened isles should bring forth rats![2]
Rocky tips, the eye of the fountain—who is their master now?
My thoughts hover about them like moths about a flame.

1. The note is by Michizane himself. Lord Minamoto was Minamoto no Tsutomu, brother of the famous Minamoto no Tōru; he died in 881. His mansion was located at Shichijō Nishi-ōmiya.
2. References to Chinese folk beliefs on the spontaneous transformation and production of beings.

✑ Dreaming of Amaro

(Written in 883. *Kanke bunsō* 2)

✑ Since Amaro died I cannot sleep at night;
if I do, I meet him in dreams and tears come coursing down.
Last summer he was over three feet tall;
this year he would have been seven years old.
He was diligent and wanted to know how to be a good son,
read his books and recited by heart the "Poem on the Capital." [1]
Medicine stayed the bitter pain, but only for ten days;
then the wind took his wandering soul off to the Nine Springs.
Since then, I hate the gods and buddhas;
better if they had never made heaven and earth!
I stare at my knees, often laugh in bitterness,
grieve for your little brother too, buried in an infant's
    grave . . .[2]
How can I bear to hear your sisters call your name, searching;
to see your mother waste away her life in grief!
For a while I thought the ache in my bowels had mended;
now suddenly it comes boiling up again.
Your mulberry bow over the door, the mugwort arrows;
your stilts by the hedge top, the riding whip of vine;

1. A long poem on the city of Ch'ang-an by the 7th cen. T'ang poet Lo
Pin-wang; according to contemporary sources, it was used in Japan as a
text for little boys learning to read Chinese.
2. A note by the poet says that Amaro's little brother died shortly
after. Two lines of very uncertain meaning have been omitted at this
point; they are philosophical in purport and apparently refer to the
transitory nature of human life.

in the garden the flower seeds we planted in fun;
on the wall, words you'd learned, your scribblings beside
    them—
each time I recall your voice, your laugh, you are here again;
then I hardly see you day or night and all becomes a daze.
A million missteps in this realm of Sumeru,
three thousand darknesses in this world of life—
O thou Bodhisattva of Mercy,
watch over my child, seat him on the great lotus!

⪦ Sudden Inspiration on a Summer Day

(*Kanke bunsō* 2)

⪦ A man free as the sky, no ties, no entanglements;
and now the rain has cleared, we get a spell of fine weather.
Three posts, more than I merit—a day to ponder that debt;
sixth day holiday, chance to relax—a time to do as I please.[1]
I lie looking at the new screen painting, a water scene;
walking, I hum cool weather poems from an old collection.
Fussy though I am by nature, I don't even mind the heat—
only there's that sadness, those dreams of Amaro.

1. Michizane at this time held the posts of Junior Assistant in the
Ministry of Ceremonies, Professor of Literature, and Acting Governor
of the province of Kaga. Officials in the Heian period were given every
sixth day off.

✍ Who Does the Cold Come Early To?

(Four from a series of ten poems using the same rhymes and initial line and describing the hardships of the common people of Sanuki, the province in Shikoku to which Michizane was appointed governor in 886. The other poems in the series deal with the vagrant, the orphan, the herb gardener, the ferryman, the salt peddler, and the wood gatherer. *Kanke bunsō* 3)

2

Who does the cold come early to?
To the peasant fled from another province.
Running away, he hoped to escape the burden of taxes;
here he's enrolled and pressed for payment once more.
Three foot coat of deer skin grown shabby,
a one room snail's house of poverty his home,
shouldering his child, wife in hand,
again and again he takes to the road to go begging.

3

Who does the cold come early to?
To the old man who lost his wife.
Tossing on his pillow, eyes wide awake,
under cramped eaves sleeping all alone.
He feels a sickness coming on, adding to his worries;
hunger threatens, but who cares if he is poor?
Hugging in his arms the motherless child,
again and again he weeps through the night.

6

Who does the cold come early to?
To the relay station house attendant.

93

Days at a time he forgets what a proper meal tastes like;
all year long, travelers to see off,
in an unlined robe, catching cold in the wind;
should he quit his job, poverty lurks in wait.
If his horses are too scrawny and slow to make the run,
again and again he's the one will feel the lash!

8

Who does the cold come early to?
It comes early to the fisherman.
The land brings forth no bounty for him;
in his little boat alone he grows old.
He hauls the line gently, always fearful it may break,
tosses the bait, but never ceases to be poor.
Hoping to peddle enough to cover taxes,
again and again he gauges the wind and the sky.

New Years Day at the Official Lodge; I Invite Guests to Join Me in a Drink

(New Years Day, 887, in Sanuki. *Kanke bunsō* 3)

I've called in guests from the seaside village for a cup of New Years wine,
though as host I feel more than ever what it means to be far from home.
I tell my boys to take just a sip, then hurry to serve the others;
village elders, after numerous rounds, still call for penalties when the cup is slow.[1]
Sorrow and sadness last year, parting hands in farewell;
today a face all smiles, relaxing my frown.
The way they tumble into carts, I know they're not just pretending to be drunk.
They've gone off and left their oars and fishing poles behind!

1. Drinkers who were slow to pass along the wine container had to drink an extra cup in penalty, a merry Chinese custom which had apparently been imported to Japan at this time. As the previous line indicates, Michizane had one or two of his sons with him, though most of his children remained in Kyoto with his wife.

✒ On the Road I Met a White-haired Old Man

(887 in Sanuki. The poem, though clearly modeled on Po Chü-i's "New Yüeh-fu" ballads, deals entirely with events in Sanuki. *Kanke bunsō* 3)

✒ On the road I met a white-haired old man,
hair white as snow, but a face still ruddy.
"Ninety-eight years I've lived," he said,
"no wife, no children, skimping along alone,
in a three-room thatched hut at the foot of South Mountain,
in cloud and mist, not farming, not trading;
the wealth in my house? one chest of cypress;
and what's inside it? one bamboo hamper."
When white-haired had finished his tale, I asked,
"What secret art is this—a ruddy face at your age?
No wife or children, no wealth either,
tell me how you keep up such spirit, such a face and form?"
White-haired put aside his stick, bowed before my horse,
courteously replied, "I'll tell you the reason:
In the late years of Jōgan, beginning of Gangyō,[1]
the government had no mercy or love, laws too often unjust.
Though drought plagued us, no word of it went to the capital;
though our people died of contagion, no one pitied or cared;
40,000 homesteads or more overrun with thorns and brambles,
eleven districts where no smoke of cooking fires rose.
Then they sent to the government office a man of the Abe clan

---

1. The Jōgan era (859–76) comprised the reign of Emperor Seiwa, the Gangyō era (877–84) that of Emperor Yōzei.

who rushed about day and night inspecting towns and villages; [2]
as word spread abroad, those who had fled came home;
relief and succor extended to all, the weary were raised up.
Once more officials and commoners honored their superiors;
aged and infant were cared for, mothers no longer abandoned
their children.
After that, we got a governor named Hō; [3]
he governed lying down, but his justice flooded the whole land.
In spring we didn't think of spring, but spring was everywhere;
fall we didn't fret about fall, and fall gave us fat harvests;
two Heavens over us,[4] five suits to wear—the roads rang with
praise;
plenty of millet, double ears of grain! was the cry from every
lane.
An old fool, I was lucky enough to enjoy their blessing;
no wife, no longer a farmer, I could still live content.
With clothes for every hamlet, our bodies were comfortably
warm;
grain to supply each region, our mouths never lacked food.
Such was the joy we knew, all worry and grief cut off;
no more care in our hearts, muscles grew stronger than ever.
Before I noticed it, frost had crept over my temples,
but the glow of the peach flower still lingers in my face."
When I had listened to the words of the white-haired old man,
I thanked him, sent him on his way, pondering to myself:
Abe has been to me a righteous elder brother,
Hō has shown me the kindness of a father.

2. Presumably Abe no Okiyuki, who was appointed *suke* or assistant
governor of Sanuki in 878.
3. Fujiwara no Hōsoku (Yasunori), appointed governor of Sanuki in
882.
4. The two wise governors.

Father and brother bequeathed me a heritage of love:
may I build on this store of goodness and learn to govern well!
Yet how hard it is to keep up old ways
when autumn moon and spring winds do not come in season!
I try to match Abe's diligence, but I get too weary;
yet my years won't permit me to "govern lying down."
And there are other things in the government hard not to
    change;
still I rush around, and in spare moments work at my poems.

✍ When I Reached the Post Station at Kaya, I Was Moved to Tears

(887; Kaya was a post station on the Yodo River south of Kyoto. Michizane was on his way from Sanuki for a visit to the capital. Mr. Wang of the poem was presumably the descendant of an immigrant family from China, Pohai, or Paekche. *Kanke bunsō* 3)

✍ Last year my old friend, His Excellency Wang,
in the post house tower gripped my hand, wept when we
    parted.
Arriving, I inquire of the official in charge;
"Some time ago," he answers, "—that little grave there."

✍ Surprised by Winter

(888, in Sanuki. *Kanke bunsō* 4)

✍ Only yesterday I sent winter away and now it's back again:
I think the heat and cold must have sprouted wings!
Roll up and put away the green bamboo bed mat,
open the chest, unpack the white wadded robe—
I don't mind that my bad record condemns me to three years
    provincial duty,
only sigh that all my life everything goes wrong.
The weather's right for the season, but my heart is full of pain,[1]
heaven's times and my times going in different directions.

1. The first part of the line alludes to the unseasonable drought that
plagued the Sanuki area in the preceding summer, and by this time had
ended.

⚄ Weeping for My Elder in Poetry Shimada

(891; on the death of his father-in-law Shimada no Tadaomi, a scholar, poet, and one of Michizane's closest friends; he and Michizane exchanged poems on numerous occasions. *Kanke bunsō* 5)

⚄ Weeping as though for a parent, bitter as a dose of herbs,
never more to share with you life's sunny spells and rains.
Not you so much I grieve for, grieving for myself;
not the dead alone mourning, but lonely ones left behind.
Fame worth ten thousand in gold will not quickly turn to ashes,
but a poor man's three-path cottage—weeds and brambles will
    claim it now.[1]
From now on, in spring wind, under an autumn moon,
poets in name only, no more the real thing.

1. A reference to the country home of the Chinese poet T'ao Yüan-ming (364–427), with its three little garden paths.

✍ On Vacation: a Poem to Record My Thoughts

(892, in Kyoto. As mentioned earlier, officials were given every sixth day off from work, but those of higher rank could on occasion request a five-day leave. *Kanke bunsō* 5)

✍ I put in for a five-day leave,
a little vacation from early duty at the office.
And during my leave where do I stay?
At my home in the Sempū Ward.
Gates bolted, no one comes to call;
the bridge broken, no horses pass by.[1]
Up early, I call the boy
to prop up the last of the chrysanthemums.
As the sun climbs higher, I urge the old groom
to sweep and tidy the sand in the garden.
At twilight I take a turn by the eastern fence,
try to wash and dust it, but the bamboo topples over.
When evening comes, I begin thinking of my books,
in rue-scented silk covers, five cartloads.[2]
Spotting the volumes I need, I take them down,
making notes to add on items overlooked.
The cold sound of fallen leaves by the stairs,
in dawn breath, flowers of frost on the flagstones:

1. His house in the Sempū Ward faced west on a small stream called the Horikawa.
2. The rue was to protect the books from insects. In the 5th month of this year Michizane had presented his work on Japanese history entitled *Ruijū kokushi* to Emperor Uda and was probably preparing additions or corrections to it.

at cockcrow I lie down, arm for a pillow,
quietly thinking, grieving for friends far away.
My girls are in the inner rooms helping their mother;
the little boy tags around after Grandpa; [3]
but I have duties that cannot be shirked,
I must leave and set out on the long road to the Palace.
One sigh brings a sinking feeling in my stomach,
a second sigh and tears begin to flow.
The east already light and still I haven't slept;
glumly I sip a cup of tea.
Heaven is indifferent to my longings for leisure;
even at home I'm busy all the time.
Karma piled up from long ages past
keeps us coming and going in these bitter lives.

3. In a poem written in Sanuki, Michizane mentions that one of his daughters had given birth to a son in the 7th month of 889, presumably this boy.

⊁ Note on My Library

(893; Michizane grumbles humorously about some of the friends and students who frequent his study. *Kanke bunsō* 7)

In Sempū Ward in the eastern sector of the capital there is a house, in the southwest corner of the house is a corridor, and at the very south end of the corridor is a room. The room is hardly more than ten feet square, so that those entering or leaving have to squeeze past each other, and those occupying the room have to sit with mats pushed together side by side. And yet out of this room in the past have come close to a hundred men who passed the *shūsai* and *shinshi* examinations. For this reason, students refer to the room as the Dragon Gate.[1] It is also called the Hill Shade Pavilion because it is west of a little hill. Near the door is a plum tree, and a few paces to the east are several clumps of bamboo. Whenever the plum flowers are in bloom or the bamboo catches the wind, it's enough to delight and brighten one's spirits and give nourishment to the soul.

When I first passed the *shūsai* examination, my father said to me, "This room is a place of distinction—while you're hard at work on your studies, it would be well to move in here."[2] Ac-

1. "To climb the Dragon Gate" is a Chinese expression meaning to succeed, particularly in the civil service examination. The men who succeeded in passing the exams were students of Michizane's father Koreyoshi, a distinguished scholar of Chinese studies who ran a kind of private academy for young men wishing to study for the civil service examinations.

2. Michizane passed the exam in 862, thus becoming a *monjō tokugyōshō* or candidate for the highest degree, that of *shinshi* or *monjōshō*.

cordingly I shifted the blinds and mats around and straightened up the room, and brought my books and stacked them away there. But alas, when space is cramped and narrow, feelings become mean and timorous. Among my various friends and acquaintances, there are some I am very close to, and some I feel I hardly know. There are some who, though at heart they don't care for me at all, always wear a pleasant expression, and some who, though as suspicious as peasants, address me in a very familiar way. There are others who, claiming that they are seeking enlightenment, go poking and prying among my private books and papers, and others who, announcing that they have come to pay a call, barge in when I am trying to rest.

Another thing—a brush is an implement for writing, and a scraper a tool for scratching out mistakes. But some of that flock of crows who descend on me, apparently unaware of the proper use for such implements, pick up the scraper and immediately start hacking at the desks, or fiddle with the brush until they've spattered and soiled my books. On top of this, in scholarship the most important thing is to gather data, and to gather data one has first of all to take notes. But since I am not a person of very proper or methodical nature, I often find I have to lay down my brush in the midst of my researches, and at such times I leave a lot of little slips of paper lying about with notes on them concerning the data I have collected. At such times people come wandering into my library without permission and, though what they're thinking about I can't imagine, the clever ones, when they spy my notes, fold them up and stuff them into the breast of their robe, and the stupid ones pick them up, tear them in two, and throw them away! Occurrences like this distress me intensely, and in addition there are countless petty little annoyances I could mention. One more thing—there are times when one of my friends for some reason comes to see me on important business. But after he has entered my library, one of the idle intruders, not bothering to ascertain whether someone with important business has entered ahead of him, comes marching straight in with his wholly unimportant affairs—it's enough to make one despair, I say; enough to make one despair!

When Lord Tung lowered the curtain, and Master Hsüeh climbed over the wall, it was not only because they wanted to concentrate on their studies—they also wanted a little peace and quiet.[3] In writing this note of mine now, I certainly don't mean to proclaim that I am breaking off all my social relations—I simply want to pour out some of my worries in writing. I am particularly ashamed to think that I have been unable to establish the kind of unofficial academy that would attract real men of worth, but instead am reduced to laying down regulations to keep uninvited intruders out of my library. Such remarks are intended only for those who do not really understand me, though those who do understand me number only about three. I hope in spreading a small net to keep out swallows and sparrows I won't be driving any phoenixes away.

Written in fear and trepidation on the first day of the seventh month of the year Mizu-no-to Ushi, Kampyō fifth year (893).

3. Tung Chung-shu (179?–104?), a leading Confucian philosopher of the Han, had so many students that he lowered the curtains of his room and lectured only to a select group of advanced students, leaving them to pass on his lectures to the beginners. I have been unable to identify the allusion to Master Hsüeh.

✍ The Spider

(Written in 895. *Kanke bunsō* 5)

✍ There is craft in this smallest insect,
with strands of web spinning out his thoughts;
in his tiny body finding rest,
and with the wind lightly turning.
Before the eaves he stakes out his broad earth;
for a moment on the hedge top lives through his life.
The ten thousand things should all be thus,
the way the Creator meant us to be.

✍ On Lo-tien's Poem on the Three Friends of the Northern Window

(Written in 901 at the official lodge at the Dazaifu in Kyushu, where Michizane was exiled in the first month of the year. He is referring to a poem by Po Lo-t'ien or Po Chü-i (772–846), included in the ten chapters of poems written when the poet was living in Lo-yang, in which he speaks of his "three friends of the northern window," the *ch'in* or horizontal lute, poetry, and wine. *Kanke kōshū*)

✍ In Mr. Po's ten chapters of Lo-yang poems
there's a poem on his three friends of the northern window,
one friend a lute to pluck, one friend wine,
but neither wine nor lute are known to me.
Though I don't know them, I manage quite well,
manage quite well without a doubt.
What is wine made of? malt mixed with water;
what are lutes made of? paulownia stretched with strings;
but why wear out fingers plucking through a piece,
why ten cups before you can relax a frown?
My acquaintance with these gentlemen has been slight indeed,
though I wish them luck, bow low in farewell.
Friend poetry stays by my side, a friend true to death,
from my grandfather's to my grandsons' time, ever loyal.
Only I'd hate to have people strolling about singing my songs;
without intoning out loud, I mull them over in my mind.[1]
My position calls for caution in what I say, and I've no new
    ideas,

1. A joking reference to the wide popularity enjoyed by Po Chü-i's poems, which in China were often set to music.

but phrases come to my lips, excerpts from old poems:
old poems—where can I find a peaceful spot to pick out favor-
    ites?
In a government lodge, three spans wide, white rushes for
    thatch.
Narrow enough, still it's aligned correctly north and south,
plain in build, but fitted with proper windows and doors.
Naturally my room too has a northern window,
a quiet place to receive him when my good friend poetry calls.
No wine, no lute—what have I plenty of?
The purple swallow's children, the yellow sparrow's chicks.
Swallow and sparrow, different species, alike in their care for
    life,
male and female guarding the nest, helping each other by turns;
they've grown accustomed to the burning of incense, offerings
    of flowers;
They don't mind when I chant sutras, call the Buddha's name.
I admire their lack of suspicion, their lack of dread,
and know they'll neither harm me nor pay me any heed;
nam-nam, tsek-tsek—as though they were speaking words;
one bug, one kernel, and they manage to stave off hunger.
They're only tiny birds, I a Confucian scholar,
yet I'm no match for them in tenderness and love.
Council of State, Official of the Right, former bearer of a seal; [2]
Assistant in the Ministry of Ceremonies, recently robed in red; [3]

2. Michizane's eldest son Takami, formerly *ushōben*, now demoted to a
post in the province of Tosa.
3. Michizane's second son Kageyuki, formerly Shikibu *taijō*, now exiled to Echigo; the red robes were those of the Fifth Rank, to which he
had been elevated.

Palace attendant with perfumed breath, abruptly dismissed from
the hall; [4]
university student plying a brush, curtains of his study still
lowered: [5]
since the imperial envoys hurried them all away,
father and sons at one time scattered in five different lands.
My mouth cannot speak, blood fills my eyes;
I look up to the gods of Heaven, down to the spirits of earth.
Drifting east, drifting west, clouds distant and vast;
second month, third month, days grown mild and long:
so many barriers closely guarded, no news gets through;
I sleep alone in bitterness, dreams seldom come.
Each step west, more mountain and river vastness to block me
from home;
each stretch of road surrounds me with new landscapes of de-
spair.
My place of exile reached in safety, who's to share my meals?
If I live till autumn winds come, I've no clothes for the cold.
Once a man had three friends, lived a life of joy;
now a man has three friends, lives a life of care; [6]
past and present differ, never two the same,
Lo-t'ien in his joy, I in sorrow—the heart makes it so.

4. Michizane's third son Kanemochi, formerly *kurōdo*, now exiled to
Ōmi; officials attending the emperor perfumed their breath by chewing
spices.
5. Michizane's fourth son Atsumochi, a *shūsai* or *monjō tokugyōshō* (see
p. 104, n. 2), now exiled to Harima.
6. Michizane's three friends are presumably poetry, the swallows, and
the sparrows.

✍ On Not Going Out the Gate

(901; the second couplet, we are told, was highly admired by Michizane's contemporaries. Though he states that he was subjected to no restrictions, his movements were nevertheless closely watched by the government. *Kanke kōshū*)

✍ Since I was demoted and exiled and live in a shack
I crouch and cringe with ten thousand fears of death.
Government office tower—I can just see the tint of its tiles;
Kannon Temple—I can only hear the sound of its bell.
Feelings inside me—let them depart with the lonely cloud;
the outside world goes on—here's a full moon to greet me.
In this place, though I'm subject to no bonds or restrictions,
what possible reason would I have for stepping out the gate?

✍ Ninth Month, Tenth Day

(Written in 901. *Kanke kōshū*)

✍ This night last year, attending at the Seiryō Palace,
I spoke of my sorrow in a "Poem on Autumn Thoughts." [1]
The robe His Majesty bestowed on me, here with me now—
each day I lift it reverently, bow to its lingering fragrance.

1. The "Poem on Autumn Thoughts," (*Kanke kōshū*), written on a theme set by Emperor Daigo, expressed Michizane's uneasiness at the honors bestowed upon him and the great difference in age between himself and the sixteen-year-old ruler, as though he had a premonition of the disaster about to befall him in the following year. The present poem is one of Michizane's most admired works, principally because of the reverence it expresses toward the sovereign. Professor Kawaguchi points out that it bears a close resemblance to a poem in 7-character *lü-shih* form by Tu Fu, the second of two poems entitled "Expressing Elation at the Winter Solstice" written in 758. In general Tu Fu's works seem to have been very little known in Japan in the Heian period, however, and the resemblance may quite possibly be coincidental.

✍ To Comfort My Little Son and Daughter

(901; all of Michizane's older daughters remained in Kyoto, while his older sons, as we have seen in a poem above, were exiled to other provinces. Only his two youngest children were allowed to accompany their father to his place of exile in Kyushu. *Kanke kōshū*)

✍ Your sisters all must stay at home,
your brothers are sent away.
Just we three together, my little children,
shall chat as we go along.
Each day we have our meals before us,
at night we sleep all together.
We have lamps and tapers to peer in the dark,
and warm clothes for the cold.
In past years you saw how the Counsellor's son
fell out of favor in the capital;
now people say he's a ragged gambler,
and call him names on the street.[1]
You've seen the barefooted wandering musician
the townspeople call the Justice's Miss—
her father, too, was a great official;
they were all in their day exceedingly rich.
Once their gold was like sand in the sea;
now they have barely enough to eat.
When you look, my children, at other people,
you can see how kind Heaven has been!

1. Yoshiomi, son of the Dainagon Nanbuchi no Toshina; he lost his post as an official sometime after 887 and drifted into the life of a gambler.

113

✒ Reading a Letter from Home

(Written in 902. *Kanke kōshū*)

✒ Three lonely months and more without news—
now a favorable wind blows me a letter.
"Someone made off with the tree by the western gate.
Strangers have set up camp in that lot in the north garden."
Ginger wrapped in a paper marked MEDICINE,
a bamboo packet of seaweed "for fasting days."
Not a word of the hunger and cold my wife and children must
   be suffering—
she didn't mean it that way, but I worry all the more.

✍ On a Snowy Night Thinking of the Bamboos at Home

(Written in 902. *Kanke kōshū*)

✍ Since I was suddenly sent away
I had to leave you far behind;
between this western outpost and the eastern hedge at home
barriers and mountains cut off all word.
Not only does the earth yawn between us,
but we must face the sharp chills of heaven.
Unable to sleep, I fret in silence
at the flurry and tumble of an all-night snow.
Nearby I watch white-thatched roofs being buried;
far away I know your jade-sleek stalks must be breaking.
The old family servant ran off long ago—
who will brave the cold to sweep your branches clean?
Upright by nature, you bend in confusion;
holding firm, you are mercilessly cracked and broken.
Your tall stalks would have made fine fishing poles—
I'm sorry I didn't cut them sooner;
short ones were just right for writing slips—
a pity I didn't long ago whittle them into shape.
With writing slips to fondle, fishing poles to dip,
how unbearably happy life might have been!
No matter how many times I say it, it's useless now,
and only brings more tears and sighs.
Though I cannot be there to prop them up,
I know my bamboos will never forsake their constant green.

115

✍ Plum Blossoms

(Written in 902. *Kanke kōshū*)

✍ The ones newly planted north of Sempū Ward,
the ones at banquet time west of Jijū Palace:
different plums, though the same man sang to them—
how the flowers must have laughed at all my grieving! ¹

1. My rendering of the last line follows one possible reading and interpretation put forward by Japanese scholars. Another interpretation, which gives the line a much more self-pitying tone, would take it to mean: "the flowers alone laugh, while I have all these griefs!"

🍃 Planting Chrysanthemums

(Written in 902. *Kanke kōshū*)

🍃 Little leaves green-skinned, white-toothed roots,
before my thatched home, hugging close to the eaves:
for them I traded cloth at the widow's house nearby,
sent a letter begging cuttings from an old monk's garden.
When I planted them I never thought of Yüan-liang,[1]
just some flowers, when they bloom, to offer to the Buddha.
These wretched days, who knows when I may die?
Pack up sand, dig a channel, weave reed fences around them!

---

1. T'ao Yüan-ming (364–427), the Chinese poet whose fondness for chrysanthemums was proverbial.

⚰ Rainy Night

(902; as may be seen, Michizane was suffering seriously from the effects of malnutrition. *Kanke kōshū*)

⚰ The hours of the spring night are not many,
the breath of spring rain should be warm,
but a man with many sorrows
finds himself at odds with the season.
When the heart is cold, the rain too is cold;
nights when you can't sleep are never short.
The gloss is gone from my skin, my bones dry up;
tears keep coming to sting my eyes;
boils and rash, beriberi in my legs—
shadows of sickness darken my whole body.
Not only does my body fail me—
the roof leaks, no boards to fix it,
dampening the clothes draped on the rack,
ruining the books and letters in their boxes.
And what of the plaints of the cook,
tending a stove where no smoke rises?
Rain may bring excess of joy to farmers;
for a stranger in exile it only means more grief.
The grief and worry form a knot in my chest;
I get up and drink a cup of tea,
drink it all, but feel no relief.
I heat a stone, try to warm the cramps in my stomach,
but this too has no effect,
and I force myself to down half a cup of wine.

118

I must think of the Emerald Radiance,[1]
think! think! put my whole heart in it!
Heaven's ways of dealing out fortune—
how can they be so unfair!

1. The Pure Land of the Emerald Radiance, presided over by the Buddha of Healing, Yakushi Nyorai.

✎ Autumn Night

(902; a note by the poet says that his little son had died. *Kanke kōshū*)

✎ In bed I toss and turn in the night's deep watches,
the dim lamp faced toward the wall; no dream comes.
Early geese, a cold cricket—these I hear as always,
but no voice of the little boy at his books.

🖎 Wind and Rain

(Written in Autumn, 902. *Kanke kōshū*)

🖎 Morning by morning the breath of the wind grows stronger;
night by night the rain sounds colder than before.
The old groom keeps asking for floss to line his robe with; [1]
in this ramshackle village, we have trouble buying fuel.
I've gotten so I don't mind how the thatched roof leaks,
only regret what the weather does to my chrysanthemums.
There must be good harvests now and then—
why is there never even a bowl of gruel to eat?

1. According to legend, an aged family retainer who accompanied Michizane into exile.

⚞ The Lamp Goes Out

(The first of two poems with this title written late in 902, a few months before the poet's death. *Kanke kōshū*)

⚞ It was not the wind—the oil is gone;
I hate the lamp that will not see me through the night.
How hard—to make ashes of the mind, to still the body!
I rise and move into the moonlight by the cold window.

APPENDIX: THE JAPANESE POETRY OF SUGAWARA NO MICHIZANE

Some 59 Japanese poems in *waka* form attributed to Michizane have been preserved. A few are included in imperial anthologies compiled close to Michizane's lifetime such as the *Kokinshū* (A.D. 905) or the *Gosenshū* (A.D. 951), and are very likely genuine. The vast majority, however, is preserved in later imperial collections such as the *Shinkokinshū* (A.D. 1205) or in the fictionalized account of Michizane's exile contained in the second chapter of the *Ōkagami*, a pseudo-historical work of doubtful date and authorship whose narrative deals with events as late as 1025.[1] It is very difficult, therefore, to determine which poems are authentic and which are later works inspired by the Michizane legend. One is tempted to read these Japanese poems attributed to Michizane in the light of his *kanshi* and to see if there are evidences that the two media influenced each other. Similarities of subject are immediately apparent, as in the works on plum and cherry blossoms and chrysanthemums, and I have noted certain other parallels in the headings below, though these may not be of any great importance. One significant point, nevertheless, emerges from the comparison—namely, the degree to which Michizane's Chinese poetry, partly due to the influence of Po Chü-i, is direct and simple in expression, and the contrasting degree to which his Japanese poetry is elliptical and requires a knowledge of the circumstances under which it was composed to be properly understood. I offer here translations of six of the more famous *waka*, the first three of which, preserved in early

1. Translated into English by Joseph K. Yamagiwa, *The Ōkagami: A Japanese Historical Tale* (London, Allen & Unwin, 1967).

collections and couched in the rather contrived style typical of his age, are almost surely genuine. The latter three, which allude in one way or another to his exile, are stylistically simpler and, in my opinion, of much less certain authenticity.

I. *Kokinshū* ch. 5. Written at a poetry contest during the Kampyō era (889–898) and describing chrysanthemums planted along the ocean in Fukiage, a beach area in Wakayama north of Wakanoura. The poem employs a device derived from Chinese and very popular in the Japanese poetry of the period in which the writer, overcome with a kind of elegant confusion of the senses, professes himself in doubt about the nature of the reality before his eyes. Michizane makes use of the same device in his *kanshi*, for example, in a poem written in 902 and entitled "Light Snow on Eastern Mountains," in which, viewing the patches of snow left on the slopes, he declares: "I mistake them for clouds lodging in the ravines, / wonder if they are cranes not yet returned to their fields."

Akikaze no	In the autumn breeze,
Fukiage ni tateru	dotting the beach at Fukiage,
Shiragiku wa	white chrysanthemums:
Hana ka aranu ka	are they blossoms, or perhaps
Nami no yosuru ka	only waves that are breaking there?

II. Probably written in 898 when Michizane accompanied the Retired Emperor Uda on a visit to Mt. Yoshino. Mt. Tamuke is in Nara, on the way to Yoshino. The *nusa* were offerings of cloth or paper to be presented to the gods of the mountain, but the poet suggests that the mountain's own garment of autumn leaves is a far more worthy offering. The poem employs word plays on *tabi* (trip / occasion); and *tamuke* (to offer / Tamuke). *Kokinshū* ch. 9. Because of its inclusion in the popular 13th cen. anthology *Hyakunin isshu*, this is among Michizane's best known works in Japanese.

Kono tabi wa   On this trip, this occasion,
Nusa mo toriaezu   offerings we bring unfit to offer,
Tamukeyama   Tamukeyama:
Momiji no nishiki   let this brocade of red leaves,
Kami no ma ni ma ni   O gods, be your gift to enjoy

III. The heading of the poem states that it was written when Michizane, accompanying the Retired Emperor Uda on a visit to Mt. Yoshino, was viewing a waterfall at the palace there. The whole poem, as will be seen, is an extended metaphor describing the waterfall, though without the heading one might well be at a loss to identify the tenor. "Unwound in water" refers to silk threads that are unraveled from cocoons that have been soaked in water. *Gosenshū* ch. 19.

Mizuhiki no	Unwound in water,
Shiraito haete	white threads
Oru hata wa	stretched on a loom;
Tabi no koromo ni	for travelers' robes,
Tachi ya kasanemu	cloth to be cut and piled in heaps

IV. Written early in 901 when Michizane took leave of the cherry trees at his home in Kyoto and set off for exile. *Gosenshū* ch. 2.

Sakurabana	Cherry flowers,
Nushi wo wasurenu	if you have not forgotten
Mono naraba	your master,
Fukikomu kaze ni	by the winds that blow
Kotozute wa seyo	send me some word, I pray!

V. Written on the same occasion as the poem above. These two poems are so close in conception as to be hardly more than variant versions of a single work, though this is by far the more famous of the two because of its inclusion in the *Ōkagami*. *Shūi-shū* ch. 16.

Kochi fukaba	When east winds blow,
Nioi okose yo	send out your fragrance,
Ume no hana	plum flowers—
Aruji nashi ni te	though masterless,
Haru na wasure so	do not forget the spring!

VI. One of the 16 poems attributed to Michizane in the *Shinko-kinshū*, this is entitled "The Sea" and is believed to have been written when Michizane was in exile and to be a profession of his guiltlessness. As the moon shines to the bottom of the clear water, no matter how deep, so will the poet's innocence be made clear to one who truly examines the facts of the case. As pointed out by Shimmura Izuru in his essay on the poem, the image of the sea in the opening line functions in a complex way, providing both a parallel to what follows—the "brimming waters" are as deep or deeper than the sea—and a contrast—unlike the sea, which is often turbulent and murky, these waters are crystal clear. (Shimmura Izuru, "On Lord Sugawara's Poem 'Not the Sea,' " *Kankō shōtokuroku*, Kyoto 1944.) The poem is found in *Shinkokinshū* ch. 18 and the *Ōkagami*. Some writers perceive Buddhist influence in the image of the brimming waters, which they identify with the primal waters that in Buddhist cosmology underlie the earth, but this allegation is doubtful. It may be of interest to note that, in a poem in Chinese written in the 9th month of 901 and entitled "Autumn Night," Michizane expresses the exact opposite view of the moon's power to reveal his innocence: "Moon bright as a mirror, yet it cannot make clear the blame; / wind sharp as a knife, yet it cannot cut through my grief."

Umi narazu   Not the sea,
Tataeru mizu no   yet to the very bottom
Soko made mo   of these brimming waters
Kiyoki kokoro wa   the moon will illumine
Tsuki zo terasamu   a blameless heart

Translations From The Oriental Classics

The Manyōshū, Nippon Gakujutsu Shinkōkai edition.
Paperback text edition.   1969

*Records of the Historian: Chapters from the Shih chi of Ssu-ma
Ch'ien*. Paperback text edition, tr. Burton Watson   1969

Cold Mountain: 100 Poems by the T'ang Poet Han-shan, tr.
Burton Watson. Also in paperback ed.   1970

Twenty Plays of the Nō Theatre, ed. Donald Keene. Also
in paperback ed.   1970

Chūshingura: The Treasury of Loyal Retainers, tr. Donald
Keene   1971

The Zen Master Hakuin: Selected Writings, tr. Philip B.
Yampolsky   1971

Chinese Rhyme-Prose, tr. Burton Watson   1971

Kūkai: Major Works, tr. Yoshito S. Hakeda   1972

*The Old Man Who Does as He Pleases: Selections from the Po-
etry and Prose of Lu Yu*, tr. Burton Watson   1973

The Lion's Roar of Queen Śrīmālā, tr. Alex & Hideko
Wayman   1974

*Courtier and Commoner in Ancient China: Selections from the
History of The Former Han by Pan Ku*, tr. Burton Wat-
son   1974

Japanese Literature in Chinese, Vol. I: *Poetry and Prose in
Chinese by Japanese Writers of the Early Period*, tr. Burton
Watson   1975

Studies In Oriental Culture

Companions To Asian Studies

Approaches to the Oriental Classics, ed. Wm. Theodore de
Bary   1959
Early Chinese Literature, by Burton Watson   1962
Approaches to Asian Civilizations, ed. Wm. Theodore de
Bary and Ainslie T. Embree   1964
The Classic Chinese Novel: A Critical Introduction, by C. T.
Hsia   1968
Chinese Lyricism: Shih Poetry from the Second to the Twelfth
Century, tr. Burton Watson   1971
A Syllabus of Indian Civilization, by Leonard A. Gordon
and Barbara Stoler Miller   1971
Twentieth-Century Chinese Stories, ed. C. T. Hsia and
Joseph S. M. Lau   1971
A Syllabus of Chinese Civilization, by J. Mason Gentzler,
2d ed.   1972
A Syllabus of Japanese Civilization, by H. Paul Varley, 2d
ed.   1972
An Introduction to Chinese Civilization, ed. John Meskill,
with the assistance of J. Mason Gentzler   1973
An Introduction to Japanese Civilization, ed. Arthur E.
Tiedemann   1974
A Guide to Oriental Classics, ed. Wm. Theodore de Bary
and Ainslie T. Embree, 2d ed.   1975

Introduction To Oriental Civilizations

Wm. Theodore de Bary, *Editor*

Sources of Japanese Tradition   1958   Paperback ed., 2 vols.   1964
Sources of Indian Tradition   1958   Paperback ed., 2 vols.   1964
Sources of Chinese Tradition   1960   Paperback ed., 2 vols.   1964